S0-BZH-629

Mr. Pasta's
Healthy Pasta
Cookbook

Mr. Pasta's Healthy Pasta Cookbook

More Than 150 Delicious, Low-Fat Pastas,
Pasta Sauces, and Pasta Meals!

Rick Rodgers

Quill

WILLIAM MORROW

New York

Copyright © 1994 by Rick Rodgers and Bill Adler Books, Inc.

All rights reserved. No part of this book may be reproduced or utilized in any form or by any means, electronic or mechanical, including photocopying, recording, or by any information storage or retrieval system, without permission in writing from the Publisher. Inquiries should be addressed to Permissions Department, William Morrow and Company, Inc., 1350 Avenue of Americas, New York, N.Y. 10019.

It is the policy of William Morrow and Company, Inc., and its imprints and affiliates, recognizing the importance of preserving what has been written, to print the books we publish on acid-free paper, and we exert our best efforts to that end.

Library of Congress Cataloging-in-Publication Data

Rodgers, Rick, 1953–
Mr. Pasta's healthy pasta cookbook : more than 150 delicious,
low-fat pastas, pasta sauces, and pasta meals! / Rick Rodgers.
p.   cm.
Includes index.
ISBN 0-688-14953-7
1. Cookery (Pasta)   I. Title.   II. Title: Healthy pasta cookbook.
TX809.M17R63   1994

641.8'22—dc22   94-6664
CIP

Printed in the United States of America

First Quill Edition

1 3 5 7 9 10 8 6 4 2

BOOK DESIGN BY GIORGETTA BELL MCREE

CONTENTS

v

FOREWORD

This is a collection of pasta recipes designed to fit the needs of today's cooks, who want quick, accessible dishes that can be prepared with a minimum of fuss and bother. But these recipes offer more. They are also low in fat and high in valuable vitamins and minerals. These dishes will nourish your family with good, wholesome foods that *taste wonderful*!

This is not a "health food" book. I don't insist that you use only whole-grain pastas (although they are good) and top every dish with tofu and bean sprouts (although they are good, too). The recipes here are sure to appeal to the confirmed meat-and-potatoes type of pasta lover as well as to the more adventuresome eater. But they are lower in fat and calories than pasta dishes of days gone by.

Because I wanted this book to appeal to the home cook without a lot of extra time, I have not included recipes for labor-intensive filled raviolis and gnocchi. The only dishes that require much time are the pasta casseroles, such as lasagne—and these can be made ahead of time, and frozen if necessary. Most recipes are for pastas that cook in minutes and are tossed with sauces that took only a little longer to prepare.

Nothing compares with the silky texture of homemade pasta, but this is not just a book about making your own. I have included some recipes for handmade pastas (using hand-cranked and electric machines) for those who like to make it from scratch, but you will have terrific success using packaged supermarket-variety dried pasta or store-bought fresh pasta. The pasta products now available are very, very good.

I believe strongly in the message this book delivers: We can eat healthfully and well with only a little planning—and not a lot of expense. Pasta, a complex carbohydrate and therefore a food we should all eat by the bowlful, is also incredibly versatile, inexpensive, and fast and easy to prepare. Who could ask for more?

ACKNOWLEDGMENTS

Diane Kniss has been at my side for every one of my cookbooks, clearing the path of the obstacles of daily life so I can have an uncluttered mental space to create recipes. Along with the first ancient cooks who invented pasta, this book owes its existence to her irreplaceable friendship and hard work. My dear friend Judith Dunbar Hines was cooking so much with us that it seemed easier for her to simply move into my apartment for a couple of weeks. And so she did, bringing dedication and professionalism, as well as supplying more than a few laughs. Thanks too to Paula Frazier and Jackie Bobrow for their helping hands. Mary Goodbody, another respected colleague who I value as a friend, did a thorough job of honing my writing into clear prose. I was very lucky to have the talented Barbara Durbin to do the recipes' nutritional analyses, as well as contribute thoughtful suggestions. The cover photograph is the work of the excellent photographer Tony Loew and the food stylist Annette Apricena. Jim Mellgren of Dean & Deluca was very generous to provide us with such stylish cookware.

A number of housewares experts gave freely of their time and expertise: Karl Schroeder, Julie Chulnick, Liz Klinga of Cuisinart, and Arlene Ward of Adventures in Cooking. Thanks to you all.

At William Morrow, I am always happy to work with Will Schwalbe, Zachary Schisgal, Judith Sutton, and Scott Manning, who offer their authors strong direction and good spirits in equal measure. To my agent, Susan Ginsburg, a final note of appreciation for her constant attention to my professional and personal well-being.

Mr. Pasta's Healthy Pasta Cookbook

Pasta Perfect

What would we do without pasta? We have come to love it with an abiding passion challenged only by our love affairs with hamburgers and with pizza. Without doubt, the home cook of the 1990s relies on pasta far more than did the home cook of the 50s and 60s. In those bygone days, spaghetti and meatballs was still considered "Italian," fed to the kids on the nights when the baby-sitter was in charge. Nowadays, we set pasta on the supper table three, four, or more times a week—and everyone is happy!

Pasta can be prepared in innumerable ways. In fact, you could serve it every day of the year and never repeat yourself. It's no longer linked in our collective mind exclusively with its Italian heritage. We're as familiar with Chinese *lo mein* and Thai *pad* as we are with good old American macaroni and cheese and red-sauced lasagne (well, *almost* as familiar!). Young children, teens, twenty-somethings, baby boomers, and grandparents all love pasta. It's inexpensive, stores well, is easy and fast to prepare, and, guess what? It's good for you, too.

PASTA AS HEALTH FOOD

Pasta is jammed with vitamins, including niacin, thiamine, and riboflavin, and minerals, such as calcium and iron. It's also low in sodium. A two-ounce unsauced serving (the per-person amount I recommend in most of my recipes) provides 190 calories, 39 milligrams of carbohydrates, 7 grams of protein, and 1 gram of fat.

What all this means is that pasta is one of the best foods you can eat. It's a grain food, made primarily from wheat flour and therefore loaded with the complex carbohydrates nutritionists and doctors say we should eat more of. Like bread, it fills you up without filling you out and supplies the body with needed energy-giving calories that are easy to burn and hard to store. (Fat calories are the opposite: hard to burn and easy to store—usually around the waist.) We have learned over the past few decades that foods high in complex carbohydrates, such as pasta, are not fattening by themselves. They are perceived as being fattening because of the oil-laden sauces, butter, cheeses, and sour cream with which we traditionally serve them.

No wonder a visit to the local Italian restaurant is often a diet-blowing experience. Think of the butter-drenched garlic bread, the sausage-and-tomato sauce showered with grated Parmesan, and the green salad swimming in oil-based dressing and "garnished" with slices of pepperoni and salami. Never mind the spumoni! But this does not have to be the case.

Italian restaurants, like many other types of restaurants all across the country, are revising their menus and offering lighter fare. This may translate to whole wheat bread sticks, plates of fresh vegetables, and an infinite variety of pastas made with intriguing seasonings, either kneaded directly into the pasta dough or incorporated in a light sauce. Of course, Italians will readily point out that this is how they have always eaten on a daily basis. They save the really rich, fatty foods for celebrations and holidays. Americans, on the other hand, are not known for reserving fattening foods for special occasions. As a nation, we consume between 37 and 45 percent of our daily calories as fat—far higher than the recommendations of the USDA, which says we should get 30 percent or less of our calories from fat.

The restaurant revolution is good news for health-conscious pasta lovers who like to dine out. The news for home cooks is equally good. Recipes abound for healthy ways to prepare pasta, as the following pages demonstrate over and over again.

WHY I AM MR. PASTA

I am a cook who, because of concern for my own health and a keen interest in learning more about healthful cooking for professional reasons, has come to appreciate the many benefits of pasta. I eat it frequently as part of my own health regimen; I develop recipes using it for the many books I work on, "pasta books" or not; and I have made one pasta dish after another for my catering clients.

During my ten years as a caterer in Manhattan, I served literally hundreds of different pastas. There are few cities with the ethnic mix of New York and my clientele reflected this delicious melting pot. For French businessmen, I might have prepared elegant ravioli *fraîches* stuffed with seafood mousse and served in saffron-scented broth; for a wedding luncheon, I might have prepared Shellfish and Mushroom Lasagne (page 128). I always set out at least two or three pasta salads on the buffet table and often even used deep-fried lengths of spaghetti as edible cocktail picks. Jokingly, I became known as "Mr. Pasta" or "Rick, the Pasta Man." My friends used to kid me that our company's motto was "Another day, another pasta."

With a stern warning from my doctor and a finger on a very obvious trend, I began revising my favorite pasta dishes to make them lower in fat. It was a labor of love filled with the joy of new discovery. These dishes tasted great! Along with this new interest in healthful eating, I also renewed my enthusiasm for working out regularly and, without really trying, began shedding pounds. Naturally, this led me to develop new recipes for exciting and healthful pasta dishes that, accompanied by a green salad with a low-fat dressing and a loaf of whole-grain bread, make a filling and wonderfully satisfying meal.

I have written this book to share these fantastic recipes with you. I have also written it to share what I have learned over the past few years about healthful cooking and eating. It's true: Crash diets don't work. What does work is a commitment to sensible, healthy eating, regular exercise, and enough appreciation for good food to cook it yourself—without relying more than necessary on the fast-food joint down the street.

PASTA AS A MAJOR FOOD GROUP

I could also call this section "From Pies to Pyramids," because that describes where nutritionists have taken us from the time we were kids until today. The nutrition chart that hung in my elementary school classroom was a circle divided into wedges, like a pie, that showed as clear as day that meat and dairy products should make up the major part of our diet. "Eat burgers and milkshakes, kids, and grow up to be big and strong," was the message. Almost as an afterthought, tiny slices of the pie reminded us to eat fruits, grains, and vegetables every now and then.

How times have changed. Today, the federal government's food pyramid shows, also as clear as day, that grains (pasta, cereal, bread, and rice) should make up the largest portion of our diet, as they form the broad base of the pyramid. Next come vegetables and fruits, and way up toward the tip (where forbidden pleasures such as fats and sweets reside) are dairy products and meats. Just the opposite of the pie.

According to the USDA, to maintain good health, all Americans should strive to eat the following number of servings of these foods every day:

pasta, cereal, bread, and rice	6 to 11 servings
vegetables	3 to 5 servings
fruits	2 to 4 servings
dairy products	2 to 3 servings
meat, poultry, fish, beans, eggs, and nuts	2 to 3 servings
fats, oils, and sweets	use sparingly

As I mentioned earlier, pasta is made from grain and therefore heads the list of the most desirable foods we can eat. This is no hardship for anyone. And since we should get at least 50 percent of our daily calories from carbohydrates, knowing numerous healthful ways to cook pasta is exactly right for today's health- and diet-conscious home cook. This is equally true whether you follow a strict vegetarian diet, one that restricts red meat, or one that includes all kinds of foods.

BUT WHAT ABOUT PROTEIN—AND FAT?

Since we were children we have been told that protein is good for us and that meat is the best source of protein going. However, to keep our bodies in top working order, we actually need less protein than was once believed by medical science. At the turn of the century, scientists insisted we should eat from two to three pounds of meat a day. From that excessive amount, no doubt, came the widespread belief that an all-American meal should center around a nice big piece of meat. Today we understand that we need only 12 to 20 percent of our total calories from protein, and over half of those calories should come from plant sources, such as beans and wheat, rather than from meat, which tends to be high in fat as well as protein. In countries where meat is scarce, expensive, or both, only a little is consumed at one time. These populations rely on fish and plant foods for adequate protein, and they have no trouble staying healthy.

Pasta is the ideal medium for those who want to cut down on their consumption of meat in a healthful, satisfying way. I include many recipes that call for only a little meat or poultry as well as recipes that combine pasta with fish and with vegetables, both of which provide good protein.

We also know that we need only very small amounts of fat to survive.

However, as with protein, we generally consume far too much of it. Too much fat contributes to any number of health problems, from obesity and joint disease to heart disease and diabetes.

There are three kinds of fats—saturated, monounsaturated, and polyunsaturated—and each one affects the body's cholesterol production. Monounsaturated and polyunsaturated fats are considered unsaturated. Saturated fats, derived mostly from animal products, appear to raise levels of undesirable serum cholesterol in the blood; unsaturated fats help lower total cholesterol in the blood.

Understanding fats is not exactly as easy as recognizing the differences between saturated and unsaturated fats, because there is a difference between polyunsaturated and monounsaturated fats. Polyunsaturated fats seem to lower both HDL ("good" cholesterol) levels *and* LDL ("bad" cholesterol) levels, making no distinction between the two. Monounsaturated fats lower only the "bad" LDL cholesterol levels, meaning that monounsaturated fats are preferred.

Monounsaturated fats, usually in the form of oils, are what you should choose when you cannot avoid fat. The best oils are canola, high-oleic sunflower, olive, and peanut oils. Barring these, try polyunsaturated oils such as safflower, soybean, and regular sunflower oil. Avoid saturated fats, such as butter, egg yolks, meat and poultry fats, cheese, and tropical oils like coconut and palm oil, if possible. A good way to identify most saturated fats is to remember that they are usually solid at room temperature (as in the case of butter and lard). And be aware that all fats, whether monounsaturated or not, contain about 120 calories per tablespoon and 13 grams fat. A gram of fat has 9 calories, while a gram of carbohydrate (such as pasta) contains only 4 calories.

It is important to keep your consumption of fat way down, remembering that only 30 percent or less of your daily calories should derive from fat. This means about fifty grams of fat for women and sixty for men. Naturally, these numbers vary with body type, age, and levels of activity. When you do eat fat, try to distribute it among the three types so that less than 10 percent comes from polyunsaturated fats, 10 percent (the less the better) from saturated fats, and the remainder from monounsaturated fats. And if you overload on fats one day, simply cut back for the next two or three.

We hear a lot about the percentages of calories from fat in specific foods and dishes, and while I do not put much stock in this method of figuring the amount of fat in the diet (I prefer to count grams), I have included the percentages in the nutritional analyses of these recipes. You may also notice that the new food labeling practices include this information. The reason I do not find this a very accurate way of determining fat consumption is because it can be misleading. For example, consider the recipe on page 228 for Orzo "Tabbouleh." It is made up mainly of carbohydrates but its percentage of calories from fats seems unhealthily high, even though it only contains 3 tablespoons of oil and 4 grams of fat. When calculated, this dish gets 55 percent of its calories from fat. In reality you are eating less than 2 teaspoons of oil!

TIPS FOR TRIMMING THE FAT

I am the first to admit I was just plain lazy about switching from a hit-or-miss, sometimes healthful, often not, kind of diet. But once I began to evaluate my old recipes, I quickly realized how easy it is to eat sensibly. Here are some of the ways I became a "low-fat" cook.

- Every time you make a dish, think of low-fat substitutes you could use to make it leaner.
- Comparison shop by checking labels for grams of fat—not just prices.
- Eat a variety of foods, including lots of vegetables, fruits, and grain products.
- Maintain a healthy weight.
- Use sugar only in moderation.
- Use salt only in moderation. Spices, fresh herbs, and lemon juice are good substitutes.
- If you drink alcoholic beverages, do so only in moderation.
- Select well-trimmed lean cuts of red meat, such as beef filet mignons, leg of lamb, pork tenderloin, and veal cutlets.
- Trim all visible fat from meat and poultry.
- Use ground turkey or chicken or extra-lean ground beef (less than 10 percent fat), instead of regular ground meats.
- If you want ground pork or veal, buy lean cuts and grind the meat yourself in the food processor or a meat grinder.
- Mix ground meat with plenty of vegetables or grains to extend it.
- Brown meat in a nonstick skillet without added oil or fat: Cook it and any added onions or seasonings over medium heat, stirring it until the meat loses its pink color. This takes about five minutes for a pound or so of meat. Drain off any accumulated liquid before continuing with the recipe.
- Leaving the skin on poultry contributes to juiciness, but be sure to remove and discard the skin before eating the poultry. Rub seasonings under the skin, not on it, before cooking.
- Skinless poultry parts, such as chicken and turkey breasts, are easy to cook. For optimal flavor and juiciness, cook them over medium heat, no hotter.

- Grilling or broiling is a great nonfat way to add flavor to meats and poultry.
- Make stocks, soups, and stews ahead of time so that you can refrigerate them (let them cool to room temperature before refrigerating). Any fat will solidify on top of the liquid as it chills and then can be easily skimmed or lifted off. Vegetable fats will only partially harden but also can be skimmed more easily.
- Store canned broths in the refrigerator so that fat will solidify on the surface and can be discarded.
- When sautéing vegetables, spray a nonstick skillet with a light misting of vegetable oil cooking spray. This reduces the possibility of scorching but introduces far less fat than poured oil. Cover the skillet and cook the vegetables over medium heat.
- Look for opportunities to cook vegetables or poultry in vegetable or chicken broth rather than fat (one tablespoon of monounsaturated olive oil adds more than thirteen grams of fat to a dish). For example, simmer carrots in chicken stock in a covered saucepan until they are crisp-tender, then sprinkle them with fresh herbs and serve. No need for butter.
- Use low-fat or nonfat versions of dairy products such as milk, sour cream, evaporated milk, ricotta, mozzarella, cottage cheese, and cream cheese. (For more on this subject, see page 18.)
- To switch from whole milk to skim milk, begin by buying 2% milk. After a few weeks, change to 1% milk, and then, finally, to skim milk. The gradual change will help you, and your family, adjust.
- Don't buy sweetened yogurt. Use nonfat plain yogurt and add your own fresh fruit, honey, or fruit-only preserves, which will add fewer calories.
- Choose whole-grain breads, with their higher fiber and greater nutrients, rather than white bread.
- Buy nonfat or low-fat salad dressings; but be sure to check the labels for artificial ingredients and preservatives. There are enough excellent preservative-free products on the market to satisfy every taste. Many of the dressings for the pasta salads in Chapter 11 can be made on their own and used on greens.
- Avoid nuts as snack food—they are high in fat. Chop them and use them sparingly on salads and pastas for added crunch.
- Buy low-fat or nonfat frozen yogurt desserts and sorbets. Crunchy biscotti cookies traditionally are made without a lot of butter, so they can be a good choice, too. Always consider fresh fruit in season for dessert. To dress it up, sprinkle a fruit salad with Grand Marnier, or drizzle berries with a little honey.
- Portion control is important. Use a small plate so you do not heap on food.

- If possible, eat your large meal at midday. This gives the body the rest of the day to work off the calories.

HOW TO USE THE RECIPES

This book contains more than one hundred fifty recipes for pasta. They were developed to be part of a well-balanced meal that might include a fresh green salad, loaded with veggies and tossed with a low-fat dressing, and whole-grain bread. Don't forget fruit for dessert. The food pyramid suggests two to four servings of fruit a day.

When devising these recipes, I used a pound of pasta for six to eight servings, about two to two and a half ounces each. These are good-sized portions, but if you want enough for seconds, cook more pasta (or serve fewer people).

Pasta is normally sold by the pound, although some packages hold nine or twelve ounces. I usually call for a pound of pasta in these recipes, but if you can only buy the pasta in nine- or twelve-ounce packages, simply cook two nine-ounce packages or one-and-a-half twelve-ounce packages, (or eighteen ounces total)—and don't worry about the additional two ounces of pasta. The extra fat and calories are minimal and you will have enough sauce. In the old days, I used to eat up to half a pound of pasta at one meal, but now that I exercise portion control, I feel better, look better, and never feel deprived.

If a pound of pasta is too much for your needs, I suggest choosing a recipe with a sauce that can be prepared separately and refrigerated for a few days or frozen for longer. That way, you can cook half a pound of pasta and use half the sauce, then serve the other half on another day tossed with more freshly cooked pasta.

When I find myself with leftovers, I add the cooked pasta to soup or mix it with liquid egg substitute and turn it into a frittata. Leftover pasta does not freeze well, unless it is a baked casserole or other dish such as lasagne. Cooked pasta will hold in the refrigerator for a day or so and is best reheated very gently. Before heating, add a little water or broth to replace the moisture the pasta has absorbed. Use a double boiler (particularly with cream-style sauces) or a microwave. Either of these is better for reheating pasta than a skillet or saucepan, even one set over medium-low heat.

For each recipe I have selected a particular pasta shape that lends itself to the cooking method and to the other ingredients. Long strands of pasta generally are best with smooth sauces, while tubular and shell-shaped pastas are good with chunky sauces. You can substitute one type of pasta for another, and, in most cases, may opt to replace dried with fresh, or vice versa, but for the best results I recommend staying within the specified pasta's family of shapes.

HOW TO USE THE NUTRITIONAL ANALYSES

The recipes were tested with either store-bought fresh or dried pastas, using an average of the nutritional information gathered from standard generic brands. The nutritional analyses for 2 ounces of the pastas are as follows:

DRIED PASTA

225 calories	14 percent protein	82 percent carbohydrates	4 percent fat	
	8 grams protein	45 grams carbohydrates	1 gram fat 0 cholesterol	2 milligrams sodium

FRESH PASTA

173 calories	14 percent protein	75 percent carbohydrates	11 percent fat	
	6 grams protein	32 grams carbohydrates	2 grams fat 0 cholesterol	17 milligrams sodium

If you choose to make the recipe with a homemade flavored pasta, you can still find out the nutritional analysis for the recipe: Subtract the figures above from the corresponding categories in the recipe. Then, add the figures for your choice of pasta back into the analysis.

Each analysis is for the main recipe, not the variations. The nutritional differences between the variations and the main recipes are so minimal that you can simply use the main recipes' analyses. Also, I have averaged the protein/carbohydrate/fat percentages to the nearest whole number, so the total may not always equal 100 percent.

The Pasta Cook's Healthful Kitchen

Just when you thought there was nothing new under the culinary sun, here come flavored and whole-grain pasta doughs, seasoned with herbs and spices and mixed with fresh vegetable and fruit juices. What a pleasing dimension these add to the pasta cook's repertoire! And that's not all. Both satiny and hearty Asian noodles are making their way out of tiny urban storefronts and onto supermarket shelves.

Pasta lovers appreciate silken noodles and robust shaped pastas of every origin. Many seek out unusual and authentic dried and fresh pastas nearly every time they shop; others experiment making pasta in their own kitchens. Finding "exotic" pasta is becoming increasingly easy as supermarkets jump on the speciality pasta bandwagon, offering fresh pasta, frozen pasta, and a wide array of dried pastas. For home pasta makers, it's easier than ever to buy a hand-cranked pasta machine at the local kitchen shop (finally, the shop clerk knows what you're talking about!). And the newer more expensive electric pasta machines permit the home cook to create any number of shapes beyond strands of fettuccine and linguine.

All of this is exciting and heartening for the pasta lover, but perhaps best of all is the recognition of pasta as an integral part of a healthful diet. And that is why I am so thrilled with the recipes in this book: They burst with good flavor and with good health.

CREATING THE RECIPES

Every one of these recipes was a pleasure to create. It seemed that every time I stopped by the market there was a new high-quality product available that made my task easier. I developed my pasta doughs using liquid egg substitute or egg whites, so that every type of pasta in the book is cholesterol-free. Naturally, those traditionally made with only flour and water have never had cholesterol, but for those doughs that do call for eggs, the liquid egg substitute works incredibly well.

Vegetable and fruit juicers, now standard equipment in many kitchens, make fast work of giving pasta dough a dazzling variety of flavors and colors.

As intriguing as the culinary possibilities of colored and flavored pastas are, I refrained from creating too many. A generous sampling of doughs infused with spices, herbs, and/or vegetable juices is sufficient for even the most fervent home cook. Who really needs pineapple pasta? From the more than thirty recipes for pasta included here you will find ample opportunity to be creative. And I hope they will inspire you to develop your own combinations.

THE LONG AND SHORT OF IT: A PASTA GLOSSARY

My neighborhood Italian grocer carries so many different sizes, shapes, and brands of pasta that I stopped counting after reaching one hundred and fifty. I discovered that different manufacturers sometimes give the same shape a different name, so that short twists may be called "rotini" by some companies and "fusilli" by others. Because of this confusion, I compiled the following list, which puts pastas into categories by shape. For the most part, any of the pastas in a given category can be substituted for another pasta in the same category. Jumping from category to category is a little more problematic. I do not recommend using thin strands, such as capelli d'angelo or linguine, for example, with heavy sauces. (See page 15 for more on matching pasta with sauce.)

The pastas listed here are Italian. For more on Asian pastas, see page 195. The translations on the list are literal from the Italian. The word *rigati* after the name on a box means that the pasta is ribbed or grooved.

PASTA GLOSSARY

LONG STRANDS (SPAGHETTI FAMILY)

Bucatini: Long, thick tubes, like hollow spaghetti.
Capelli d'angelo: Also called "angel hair," its English translation, or capellini. Very thin strands; take care and do not overcook.
Fusilli: Long, curly strands.
Perciatelli: Similiar to bucatini, but often slightly thicker.
Spaghetti ("lengths of cord"): Long, thin, round strand-like pasta.
Vermicelli ("little strings" or "little worms"): Very thin spaghetti, but slightly thicker than capelli d'angelo.

FLAT RIBBONS (FETTUCCINE FAMILY)

Fettuccine ("small ribbons"): Flat ribbon noodles about ¼ inch wide.
Lasagne: Very wide flat pasta, about 3 to 4 inches. Although lasagne is generally used in a baked dish, it can be tossed with sauce and served unbaked.
Linguine ("little tongue"): Ribbons of pasta cut ⅛ inch wide.
Pappardelle: Wide ribbons, about 1 inch across.
Tagliatelle: Slightly wider than fettuccine.

TUBULAR PASTAS (MACARONI FAMILY)

Mostaccioli ("little moustaches"): Tubular pasta about 2 inches long, made in plain and ribbed versions.
Penne ("quills"): Tubular pasta with the ends cut on the diagonal to resemble a quill pen.
Rigatoni: Large ribbed tubes.
Ziti ("bridegrooms"): Medium-wide tubes about 1 inch long.

SOUP PASTAS (TINY PASTAS)

Acini di pepe ("peppercorns"): Tiny pasta stubs.
Ditali ("little thimbles"): Very short macaroni.
Orzo ("barley"): This pasta looks more like rice, and is often served as a substitute.
Pastina ("tiny dough"): Very, very small flakes of pasta.

Semi di melone ("melon seeds"): Similar to orzo, but thinner.
Stelline ("little stars"): Tiny star-shaped pasta.
Tripolini: Tiny bow ties, named in honor of the battle of Tripoli.
Tubetti ("little tubes"): Short macaroni, slightly smaller than ditali.

MISCELLANEOUS SHAPES

Cavatelli: Small elongated, shell-shaped pasta.
Conchiglie ("shells"): Medium-sized shells for saucing.
Conchiglioni ("large shells"): Shells for stuffing.
Farfalle ("butterflies"): Often Americanized to "bow ties," which they
    also resemble.
Gemelli ("twins"): Two short spaghetti-like strands twisted together.
Manicotti ("Small muffs"): Large pasta tubes for stuffing.
Orecchiette ("little ears"): Plump oval discs.
Radiatore ("little radiators"): Multi-ribbed medium-sized pasta shape.
Rotelle/Rotini: Corkscrew-shaped pasta; sometimes mislabeled as "fu-
    silli."
Ruote: Wagon wheel–shaped pasta.

HOW TO COOK AND SERVE PASTA

Pasta loves to swim, so give it plenty of water. For a pound of pasta,
that ideally means a pot with a six-quart capacity, filled with five quarts
of cold water. Despite what you may have read elsewhere, *do not add salt
at this point.* Adding salt at the start increases the time the water takes to
boil and imparts an odd metallic taste to it. Cover the pot tightly and let
it come to a full boil over high heat. Then add a teaspoon of salt for every
quart of water. To avoid measuring the salt, just add salt to the water
until the water tastes slightly salty. Pasta cooked in unsalted water is flat-
tasting, but if your diet dictates it, then omit the salt.

Once the water is boiling, *gradually* add the pasta. If you submerge it
slowly, it will not clump together at the bottom of the pot; there is no
reason to add oil to the pasta water to prevent sticking. For long strands
of pasta, like spaghetti, put about a quarter at a time into the pot, gently
bending it into the water as it softens. If the water loses its boil, cover it
only until it returns to the boil, then immediately uncover the pot. Cook,
stirring occasionally to keep the pasta from sticking.

Cooking times in this book are only estimates. Dried pastas vary from brand
to brand, and the cooking time for fresh pasta depends entirely on how
long it has air-dried before taking the plunge. It may be that a watched

pot never boils, but watching the pasta pot is a very good idea, especially if the pasta is fresh. Stand close by and check the progress. Taste-test for doneness by lifting a piece from the water with tongs and biting into it. (Run the pasta under cold water before biting into it if it is too hot.) Doneness cannot be determined visually—you must get your mouth involved. In Italy, properly cooked pasta is called *al dente*, literally, "to the tooth." It should be just tender yet still slightly firm to the bite. If the pasta will be cooked further in the oven, as in a lasagne, cook it only until barely tender, keeping in mind that it will soften further during baking.

When the pasta is done, drain it in a large colander. It does not have to be drained until bone-dry; some of the water should cling to the pasta as it will help distribute the sauce. In fact, you will notice that in some recipes, I instruct you to scoop a little cooking water from the pot to mix with the sauce. But excess water can hide in the holes and crannies of tubular pastas, so give these an extra shake in the colander.

Some recipes, such as those for salads or for when the pasta is only parcooked, instruct you to rinse the pasta. But in general, do not rinse. The running water removes the starch that keeps the pasta firm and washes away valuable nutrients.

Do not let the pasta cool in the colander. Return it to the still-warm cooking pot without delay and toss it with the ready-and-waiting sauce. Otherwise, the pasta will stick. Not only does the cooking pot keep the pasta and sauce warm, it is a far less messy place to toss the pasta with the sauce than the serving bowl.

Don't let pasta get cold before serving it. Tepid pasta is never desirable. Be sure the serving bowl is warm, and, if possible, warm the individual bowls and plates too. My favorite method for warming the serving bowl is to set the bowl beneath the colander in the sink so that the hot cooking water fills the bowl when the pasta is drained. (Be sure the bowl is heatproof.) Leave the hot water in the bowl while you toss the pasta with the sauce and then, just before serving, dump out the water, wipe out the bowl, and fill it with the pasta. (Alternatively, heat the bowl in a 200°F. oven for about five minutes.) Finally, serve pasta with tongs. They are far more efficient than two spoons or the claw-shaped pasta servers.

GILDING THE LILY: MATCHING PASTAS AND SAUCES

For each recipe, I have chosen the type of pasta I think best for that sauce. There are no rules and, in the end, it comes down to personal taste, but certain pastas simply seem better suited for certain sauces than others. In Italy, no distinction is made between fresh and dried pasta in terms of quality. Both varieties are popular, and decisions are made based purely on the sauce ingredients. Following are some general guidelines to selecting the right pasta for the sauce.

- Thin pastas (such as capelli d'angelo and vermicelli) should be dressed with delicate, thin sauces. Meat sauces slip off these skinny strands and end up at the bottom of the bowl.
- Fettuccine and linguine are best for delicate sauces made with vegetables, seafood, and cream.
- Tubular pastas or dried lasagne are best for baked dishes. Fresh pastas are hard to cook to a firm al dente stage and end up overbaking in the oven. If you use fresh lasagne, barely cook it.
- Tubular pastas are best with meat sauces as the nuggets of meat nestle inside the tubes. Most of the shapes listed under "miscellaneous" on page 14 hold up well to chunky, textured sauces.

THE PASTA MAKER'S LEXICON

To perfect your pasta-cooking experience, I have assembled an alphabetical list of ingredients and utensils that will enhance your endeavor. Some will be more familiar than others, but all have a place, at one time or another, in any kitchen where pasta is regularly prepared. (I have not included hand-cranked or electric pasta machines in this list. They are described in detail in Chapters 3 and 4.)

Beans, Canned and Dried: Beans are packed with plant protein, complex carbohydrates, and fiber. When combined with pasta, their protein profile soars. Canned beans are a convenience, but dried beans contain less sodium. Be sure to rinse canned beans under warm running water for at least ten seconds to rinse off excess sodium.

Dried beans are easy to prepare, although they require time. I prefer cooking dried beans to using canned beans, as I have more control over the texture, and the resulting cooking liquid is an excellent ingredient. Buy dried beans at a store with a good turnover to ensure that they are reasonably fresh. Ancient beans will never cook to tenderness.

Rinse dried beans and pick through them to remove any stones or debris. Put them in a large bowl and add enough water to cover by three inches. Let them stand overnight at room temperature. This not only hydrates the beans, it also reduces the sugars in them that contribute to gastric discomfort.

If you do not have time to soak the beans for at least eight hours, bring them and water to cover by three inches to a boil, and cook at a rolling boil for two minutes. Remove the pot from the heat, cover, and let the beans stand for one hour. While this "quick" method is effective, the cooked beans will be firmer if allowed to soak at room temperature overnight.

After soaking (or quick-soaking), drain the beans and put them in a large saucepan with enough water to cover by two inches. Bring the water to a boil, reduce the heat to low, and simmer, uncovered, until the beans are just tender. Cooking the beans uncovered helps keep them intact and firm. Leaving the lid on will result in soft, creamy beans, which you might prefer for soups, stews, or sauces. Exactly how long the beans should cook depends on the type, size, and freshness of the beans, but count on an hour or so. (Check often for doneness often to avoid soggy, overcooked beans.) If the water cooks away, simply add more boiling water to just cover the beans. About fifteen minutes before the end of cooking, season the beans to taste with salt. Do not add it earlier, or it will toughen the beans. Drain the beans, and reserve the cooking liquid if desired.

One cup of dried beans yields about two cups of cooked beans.

Bread Crumbs, Fresh and Dried: Bread crumbs made at home will always be better than store-bought. Whenever I have leftover French or Italian bread, I turn it into crumbs to store in the freezer.

To make fresh bread crumbs, simply whirl day-old bread in a food processor fitted with the metal blade, or process in the blender in smaller batches. I leave the crust on the bread, although you may prefer to remove it. The bread crumbs will be soft and fluffy, perfect to use with pasta as a binder.

To make dried bread crumbs, begin with stale bread that is quite hard (at least two days old). Process it, with or without the crust, in a food processor or blender. Toss these crunchy crumbs with pasta.

To make dried crumbs from fresh bread, spread the crumbs on a baking sheet and bake them in a 300°F. oven for about 15 minutes, until dry but not browned. Let them cool before using.

Packaged dried bread crumbs are a poor substitute. They are sandy, not crunchy.

Chile Peppers, Hot Fresh: All chile peppers are not created equal. In general, smaller ones are hotter than larger ones. When testing these recipes, I used fresh jalapeños, which are small green peppers available in most markets. If you prefer another sort, adjust the amount to suit your taste. There is more heat in the seeds and ribs than in the flesh, which is why it is advisable to remove the seeds and ribs before using the peppers. Handle fresh chiles with care and don't let the juice or oil enter cuts or get in your eyes. Wear rubber gloves as a precaution if you wish.

Couscous: This tiny, pellet-shaped pasta is made from semolina or whole wheat flour. It is steamed, not boiled, and when cooked, resembles fluffy grains, rather than pasta. There are two versions available, traditional and quick-cooking, both products of Morocco. The recipes in this book use the quick-cooking variety.

Dairy Products, Reduced-Fat: Supermarket dairy cases are undergoing a radical change. New nonfat and reduced-fat versions of many cheeses are joining the whole milk and part-skim varieties. Before I became more familiar with low-fat cooking, I turned my nose up at these products, incorrectly assuming that their quality was "reduced" too. Admittedly, when eaten on their own, some brands may not have the identical texture and taste as their whole milk or part-skim equivalents, but when combined with other ingredients, the results are admirable.

Evaporated skimmed milk is a canned product that stands in for heavy cream in many recipes. It is thinner than heavy cream, so use it in already thickened sauces to give a creamy taste. It will not add much body. Alone, it has a slightly sweet flavor, and therefore is best combined with other full-flavored ingredients.

Farmer's cheese is a low-fat, semifirm cheese similiar to a somewhat dry, pressed cottage cheese. It is becoming more widely available and can be found packaged in the refrigerated section of most supermarkets.

Nonfat cottage cheese is one of the best new products. It has small firm curds with a pleasant and distinctive acidity.

Nonfat mozzarella cheese has a softer texture than the part-skim or whole milk versions, but mixed in a pasta casserole, it is just fine. If you have trouble shredding nonfat mozzarella, place it in the freezer until partially frozen and firm before shredding.

Nonfat ricotta cheese is fantastic in pasta dishes. It can be whirled in a blender to use in "cream" sauces. This ricotta is wetter than full-fat ricotta, so you may choose to drain some of the whey before using. It is not the same as part-skim ricotta cheese, so read the label carefully. Part-skim ricotta cheese can be used as a substitute but it has higher fat and calorie counts.

Nonfat sour cream alternative is a milder-tasting, thinner substitute for high-calorie sour cream, but the savings in fat are worth the slight compromises. Again, there are both low-fat and nonfat versions, so choose carefully.

Reduced-fat Cheddar cheese comes in mild and sharp flavors. Search out the sharp version for the best flavor.

Reduced-fat cream cheese is also called Neufchâtel, after the Swiss town that developed the original version. It is not nonfat, but it has only one third the calories of regular cream cheese. There is also a nonfat cream cheese product on the market that can be used as a substitute, if you wish.

I do not cook with nondairy tofu (soy) cheeses. I am not fond of their flavor, and they often have too much fat to be considered for low-fat cooking.

Flavoring Oils: These are really very strong flavoring extracts and should not be used as cooking oils. Add them sparingly (¼ to ½ teaspoon per 1-pound batch) to flavored pasta doughs to provide extra punch. They come in basil, chile, garlic, orange, lemon, and lime flavors. (See Mail-Order Sources, page 249.)

Flours: Flour, created from just about any grain you can imagine, is the backbone of pasta making. The most popular, of course, is wheat flour. Most of these recipes use *unbleached all-purpose flour* with a protein content of about 12 percent. Look at the nutritional information on the side of the bag to determine the protein content. The higher the protein content, the more gluten the flour contains. Gluten is the protein in flour that gives a dough strength, and pasta made from gluten-rich unbleached flour has a desirable firm texture. *Bleached all-purpose flour* is chemically treated to give it a brighter white color. This treatment reduces the gluten content to about 10 percent and decreases the nutritional value of the flour. You may use it, if necessary, but your pasta will be somewhat less firm.

Durum semolina makes the best pasta. Unfortunately, this flour needs more than a little explanation. Semolina is not a grain, nor is it technically a flour. Semolina is a specific coarse grind of durum wheat, a variety that is stronger than regular wheat, and semolina supplies the firm texture and golden color that identifies high-quality pasta. Semolina looks and feels more like cornmeal than wheat flour; it is not powdery. It is often labeled "semolina flour" or "pasta flour." Semolina is available at natural food stores, Italian grocers, or by mail order (see page 249). You can also find *durum flour* (which *is* powdery) at some specialty food stores. This a whole-grain flour and can be used in the whole-grain pasta recipes as a substitute for whole wheat flour. It makes a beige-colored pasta.

Whole-grain flours make excellent, nutritious pastas. They have varying amounts of gluten, however, and are usually combined with wheat flour to yield a strong dough. For example, *rye* has very little gluten and the dough made with it is sticky. *Buckwheat,* which is actually fruit-related, gives dough a slightly sour tang. *Kamut* is a full-flavored African variety of wheat that works quite well in pasta dough. *Spelt* has a nutty note and has the added advantage of being gluten-free. This means that wheat-intolerant people can enjoy pasta made from spelt. *Triticale* (tri-tee-KAYlee) is a hybrid of wheat and rye that combines the best flavor features of both. Kamut, spelt, and triticale flours can be used full strength, without additional wheat flour, to make wonderful pastas. All whole-wheat grains should be stored in the refrigerator, as the bran they contain can spoil easily at room temperature.

Herbs: I use *fresh herbs* whenever possible, as my greengrocer has them year-round. I encourage those of you who aren't so lucky to grow them in a window box to snip throughout the colder months. When you use fresh herbs in a sauce, add them toward the end of the simmering time because their volatile oils evaporate during long cooking.

Dried herbs have a place in the kitchen—but be sure that place is dark and cool, away from the stove. Herbs in glass jars keep better than those in little cans or plastic bags. It is a good idea to mark your herbs and spices with the date of purchase and replace them every six months. When I use dried herbs, I crush them between my fingers to release their aroma and flavor as I sprinkle them into a dish.

There is a standard "one tablespoon fresh equals one teaspoon dried" rule of thumb for herb substitutions, but I don't find this to be accurate. Taste is your best guide. There is no substitute for large measures of fresh basil (for basil pesto, for example), but luckily, fresh basil is now available year-round, at least in urban areas.

Lemongrass: This long bamboo-like herb has a lovely, citrus-like aroma and is available in Asian markets. The stalks are very tough and will only soften after mincing and lengthy simmering in a liquid. I prefer to slice a three-inch piece off the bulbous root end and split it lengthwise. A short amount of simmering releases the flavor, and the two pieces of lemongrass can easily be fished out and discarded. As a substitute, use the grated zest of one lime for this three-inch amount.

Liquid Egg Substitute: These relatively new cholesterol-free products can usually be found in the frozen food section of the supermarket. They need to be defrosted before using. There are a few newer brands of refrigerated egg substitutes, which are more convenient, so look out for them. Liquid egg substitutes are merely egg whites that have been colored with natural vegetable dyes. (Remove the yolk from the egg, and you've removed the cholesterol.) A quarter cup equals two large egg whites, which can be substituted instead in any recipe. I prefer liquid egg substitute to egg whites because I find the golden color of the egg substitute more appetizing. Also, when separated to discard the yolks, you are throwing away half of what you paid for.

Nonstick Skillets: Nonstick skillets are the low-fat cook's best friend. Their slick surfaces allow you to use very little fat in stove-top cooking. Nonstick vegetable cooking spray is usually all you need for success. The two most convenient sizes are a medium-sized skillet about 10 inches across and a large deep skillet about 14 inches across. The large skillet works as well as a wok for stir-fries. Buy the best nonstick skillets you can afford, as the surface is stronger and less apt to scratch on the better brands. Also, purchase a tight-fitting lid for each skillet (or cull them from your existing lids).

Nonstick Vegetable Cooking Spray: A short spray of this product allows you to use very little fat. Spray with a wide, sweeping motion just to mist the surface of the pan. The longer you spray, the more oil you'll use and the fat grams will climb. I buy canola oil cooking spray in an environmentally safe dispenser at a natural food store.

Olives, Mediterranean Black: Olives have plenty of fat in them, and although that fat is monounsaturated, they still add calories and fat grams to a dish. When cooking with olives, be sure to use the most flavorful, high-quality ones available. This usually means imported Mediterranean olives from Italy, France, or Spain, available in glass jars or in bulk from a specialty grocer—not canned California ripe olives. Brine-cured olives, such as Niçoise olives, are my favorites. Calamata olives, cured with vinegar so that they have a sharp taste, are not an exact substitute, but will work. To pit olives, smash them with a meat pounder or pestle, and remove the pits. The bruised condition of the olives doesn't matter, since they're going to be chopped anyway.

Olive Oil: I cook with *extra-virgin olive oil,* a golden-green oil from the first pressing of the olives. Even though this oil is more expensive than the pale gold *pure olive oil,* it has a much fuller flavor and is more versatile. Warning: "Light" olive oil is *not* light in calories, only in flavor—for culinary wimps who find olive oil "too strong" a taste for their palates. All oils, regardless of flavor, have the same amount of fat and calories per tablespoon (about 13 fat grams and 120 calories). Extra-virgin olive oil can be sparingly drizzled on vegetables instead of butter or used in small amounts in salad dressings. Try mixing one tablespoon of olive oil and two tablespoons of balsamic vinegar for an individual portion of dressing.

Buy an extra-virgin oil that is not too expensive and has a well-rounded, understated fruity taste. The pricier the oil, the more distinctive the flavor, and these special "boutique" oils are best unheated, in salads or on grilled vegetables, where their flavors can shine. Extra-virgin olive oil smokes at lower temperatures than other oils, so heat it gently. If you add vegetables to the skillet at the same time as the oil, you minimize the chances of overheating the oil. Or, use half canola oil, which has a higher smoking point, and half extra-virgin olive oil. Store extra-virgin olive oil in a cool, dark place. Or refrigerate it if you do not plan to use it within six months. The oil will cloud, but will become clear after standing at room temperature.

Parmesan Cheese: While I am willing to use nonfat alternatives of some cheeses, I will not give up the unique flavor and texture of real Italian *Parmigiano-Reggiano.* The prepackaged, pre-grated varieties bear no resemblance to the real thing. And a little of this pale-gold firm cheese goes a long way. You will find that only one tablespoon sprinkled over each serving sufficiently enhances the dish. (One tablespoon of Parmesan has about 1.5 fat grams). Be sure the cheese is from Italy, or you may end up buying an "imported" Parmesan from Argentina; real Parmesan's rind is stamped with the words "Parmigiano-Reggiano." Store the cheese in the refrigerator, tightly sealed in plastic wrap. Use a hand grater to grate the cheese just before serving.

Porcini Mushrooms, Dried: Dried porcini mushrooms lend their deep, earthy flavor to many dishes, but like all dried mushrooms, they must be prepared properly. Dried mushrooms hide a lot of grit, and nothing spoils a dish more effectively than sandy mushrooms.

Rinse the mushrooms briefly under cold water to loosen the grit, then place them in a small bowl and cover with hot water. Soak until softened, about thirty minutes. Lift the mushrooms out of the water, leaving any grit behind in the bottom of the bowl. Rinse the mushrooms again, and chop them. Pour the soaking liquid through a sieve lined with a moistened paper towel to strain out any remaining grit. There's a lot of flavor in that soaking water, so don't discard it—pour it into your sauce for a real flavor boost.

Dried mushrooms are expensive, so treat them with respect. You can substitute dried cèpes, chanterelles, or morels in most recipes. Their flavors are different but equally delicious.

Salt: While this is not a low-sodium cookbook and we now know that sodium is not the villain it was previously taken for, Americans do consume more salt than we need. You should restrict your sodium intake to 2,400 to 3,000 milligrams per day (about one teaspoon of salt)—or less if you have high blood pressure.

Salt is always a matter of personal taste. Every good cook tastes the food before it goes onto the table and seasons accordingly with salt and pepper. If you wish, leave the salt out entirely, and allow guests to season their individual servings. I keep salt in a small bowl so that I can see how much I'm using, seasoning by the pinch, not the spoonful. It is hard to gauge amounts of salt when using a shaker.

You may choose to use reduced-sodium canned tomatoes, but I find the flavor suffers, and I used regular canned tomato products in developing these recipes. I did rely on reduced-sodium soy sauce and canned chicken broth.

I use a teaspoon of salt for every quart of pasta cooking water, but the pasta absorbs such a minimal amount of sodium that it isn't accounted for in the nutritional analyses. For flavor considerations (I find unsalted pasta flat and unpalatable), I do not recommend unsalted pasta cooking water. I also have left the salt out of many pasta doughs. I use it only in recipes with ingredients (like vegetable juices or herbs) that need a little extra seasoning.

Shallots: Shallots look like small, brown-skinned onions, and taste like a cross between red onions and garlic. You can substitute either red onions or scallions if necessary, but shallots have their own individual taste that can't be duplicated. When peeled, a shallot often will turn out to be two smaller bulbs. Is that one shallot or two? I consider "one shallot" to equal three finely chopped tablespoons.

Shiitake Mushrooms, Dried: These are also called Chinese black mushrooms and are sold whole in plastic bags or in bulk in Asian markets. Rinse the mushrooms under cold running water and soak in hot water to cover until softened, about thirty minutes. The thick tough stems should be discarded, and the soaking liquid may be discarded.

Sun-dried Tomatoes: Packed in olive oil or dehydrated and loose-packed without oil, these deliver intense tomato flavor and a chewy texture. Rinse the oil-packed ones well under warm water to remove as much oil as possible. The dehydrated tomatoes need to be soaked in hot water to cover until softened, from three to thirty minutes. The range is because of the texture of the unsoaked tomato—hard, leathery ones have better flavor and less salt, and they take longer to soften. The softer ones have been treated with sulphur dioxide, and although they take less time to soften (if they need softening at all), I prefer the hard sun-dried tomatoes. Imported Italian sun-dried tomatoes are normally heavily salted. Look for a good American brand, like L'Espirit from Virginia.

Tomatoes, Fresh and Canned: Tomatoes are an important ingredient in pasta cooking. There are two types of tomatoes suitable for cooking: small *plum* (*Roma*) tomatoes and large *beefsteak* tomatoes (cherry tomatoes are best uncooked in salads). I always use ripe plum tomatoes for my sauces, as they have less juice and more body than the larger varieties. If you know you're going to want plum tomatoes to make a dish, plan ahead. Buy them a few days in advance to be sure they will be ripe. Given enough time, slightly hard tomatoes will ripen beautifully at room temperature. Let them stand, unwrapped, in a bowl on the kitchen counter or on a sunny windowsill. Never store tomatoes in the refrigerator—that's the easiest way to get mushy, mealy tomatoes.

Many a good pasta sauce has been ruined by the watery, lackluster juices given off by large beefsteak tomatoes. I reserve large tomatoes for salads or soups. If you have a profusion of very ripe large tomatoes that you must use in a sauce, add a good dose of tomato paste and be prepared to simmer them for quite a while longer than plum tomatoes for a thick consistency.

Fresh tomatoes, plum or large, should be seeded before chopping. Cut the tomato in half crosswise and squeeze gently to remove the globules of seeds (they may be coaxed out with the tip of a finger, if necessary). Make this a quick job—every seed doesn't have to come out. Many cookbooks recommend peeling the tomatoes first by blanching for about thirty seconds in a pot of boiling water, draining under running cold water to cool quickly, and then skinning with a sharp knife. I rarely bother with this tedious step, but if you have the time, you can peel your tomatoes as a refinement.

There is absolutely nothing wrong with good *canned tomatoes.* In fact, it is better to use high-quality canned tomatoes than bland, pink, hard fresh tomatoes. I like to combine the firm texture and tang of fresh plum tomatoes with the bright color and intense concentrated flavor of canned in Herbed Marinara Sauce (page 90). The best canned tomatoes come from San Marzano, Italy. Beware of imitations—many brands are labeled "imported," and emblazoned with Italianesque colors and lingo, but are imported from Israel, Mexico, or Chile. This does not mean that the other countries' tomatoes aren't acceptable, but they don't have the meaty texture and sweet-tangy flavor of the San Marzanos. The important thing is to find a brand you like and stick with it. The canned tomatoes should be a rich, dark red without any blemishes, and the juices should have some body. I use three types of canned tomatoes: tomatoes in juice, tomatoes in thick tomato puree, and crushed tomatoes. They are not easily interchangeable, so be sure you pick up the right can at the market.

Many recipes call for drained chopped tomatoes. The tomatoes can be chopped by pulsing in a food processor, but I find the easiest way is to drain the juices from the tomatoes (right into the saucepan, if the recipe calls for it), leaving the tomatoes in the can. Then reach into the can, and squeeze the tomatoes through your fingers for instant drained chopped tomatoes. Or add the tomatoes to the saucepan and use the sharp edge of a large metal spoon to chop the tomatoes in the pan. To substitute canned tomatoes for fresh, or vice versa, remember that one pound of ripe plum tomatoes equals one sixteen-ounce can of tomatoes, drained.

I like concentrated tomato paste in a tube, which can be reclosed like toothpaste and stored in the refrigerator. This eliminates those moldy, forgotten, half-used cans. This kind of tomato paste is concentrated, so use about half as much as regular paste. (I tested these recipes with the more widely available regular tomato paste.) Tomato paste in tubes is available at many supermarkets, but if you can't find it, try this trick: Spoon tablespoons of leftover canned tomato paste onto a sheet of foil, and freeze until solid. Transfer the solid globs of paste to a freezer bag and use, unthawed, when needed.

Vegetable Juices: Many of the colored pastas in this book use vegetable juices for their hues. A juice extractor does the job efficiently. However, if you don't own one, use a blender. Place about two cups finely chopped vegetables in the blender with about one cup of water. Blend until the vegetables are liquified, about one minute at high speed. Strain through a fine-mesh wire sieve into a bowl, pressing hard on the solids. The resulting liquid will color the pasta almost as brightly as pure vegetable juice from an extractor.

Vinegars: Most of us cook with wine or cider vinegars, which are very tart. Their sharp taste needs to be balanced with something bland, usually oil. By using less acidic vinegars, you can still get that nice sharp flavor but cut back or eliminate the oil in salad dressings. You can sprinkle these vinegars on dishes as a seasoning. You may have to go to a specialty grocer for them, but more and more supermarkets are stocking them.

Balsamic vinegar is dark and mellow, with a depth of flavor that comes from its long aging in wooden barrels. Made in Italy, it is available in a wide price range, from the very expensive artisan vinegars to less expensive factory-made brands. Buy the best you can afford but reserve the very pricey balsamic vinegars to drizzle sparingly as a condiment on salads or grilled meats.

Rice vinegar, used in Asian cuisines, is either plain or "seasoned." Buy the plain, as the seasoned version is mixed with sugar and salt and is meant for sushi rice.

Sherry vinegar has a slightly sweet edge. It is usually imported from Spain.

Hand-Delivered Pasta: Making Pasta by Hand

Like making bread by hand, making pasta by hand is a soul-satisfying activity guaranteed to relieve tension and produce a superior product. Classic pasta, produced for generations in both farm and city kitchens throughout Italy, is only as complicated as mixing flour and eggs on a tabletop and then rolling out the dough with a pin before cutting it into shapes. Today's cook may enlist the aid of a modern appliance or two to update the process, but the results are still classically fine. Making pasta by hand is not quick—but the result is worth every second.

There are advantages to making pasta by hand in a hand-cranked machine rather than relying on an electric pasta machine. No electric machine can duplicate the exquisite texture of handmade dough, nor will the dough be as forgiving. When made by hand, the dough's consistency can be adjusted in a few seconds with a sprinkling of flour or water—a procedure that is more complicated in a machine. Adding ingredients such as fruit juices or seeds is more challenging in an electric machine too. However, these machines allow the home cook to duplicate numerous shapes previously only possible in the factory, and they are ideal for cooks who do not feel dexterous with a rolling pin. I discuss using electric machines and provide accompanying recipes in the next chapter. Keep in mind that the recipes in this chapter were developed for hand-cranked machines (handmade pastas by definition) and *cannot* be used in an electric machine.

MAKING THE DOUGH

Handmade pasta dough can be made directly on a work surface, in a bowl, in a food processor, or in a standing electric mixer. It can also be mixed in a bread machine or a dough machine (a device that costs as much but is less versatile than a good electric mixer or food processor), but I do not recommend either for making pasta. All of the recipes in this chapter can be adapted to any of the four procedures described below. Variations are detailed in individual recipes. Some words of advice:

- Proportions of flour and liquid are always approximate, because of the varying moisture contents of different flours caused by the amount of humidity in the air and/or the exact grind or type of flour. You may find that you need to add a little more flour or water to reach the proper consistency. When there is a variable amount of liquid listed in a recipe, start with the minimum amount, and add the remainder only if needed.
- Traditional pasta doughs are made with whole eggs or egg yolks. To make these doughs cholesterol-free, I tested the recipes with liquid egg substitute. You may substitute egg whites (one large egg white equals two tablespoons liquid egg substitute) or whole eggs (one large egg equals a quarter cup of liquid egg substitute). Dough made with liquid egg substitute is stickier than classic egg pasta dough, but do not be tempted to add more flour than suggested. The dough should be firm but moist. As it stands, the flour in the dough will absorb a lot of the moisture, and the tackiness will disappear.
- Sometimes the intensity of colored and flavored pastas is not as strong as you want, especially if the pasta is made with fresh vegetable or fruit juice. (Commercial vegetable-flavored pastas are made with dehydrated vegetable powders, unavailable at present to home cooks.)

  I prefer middleweight pastas, not heavyweights. I want them to mingle with the sauce, not manhandle it! However, for those cooks who want pasta to pack more punch, there are a couple of tricks to pump up the flavor. The easiest way is to use flavoring oils (see page 19), currently available in basil, chile, garlic, lemon, lime, and orange. Mix a quarter to one half teaspoon of oil into a one-pound batch of handmade dough. Or if using vegetable or fruit juice, extract twice as much as called for in the recipe. Put it in a microwave-safe bowl or medium saucepan and, in the microwave or on top of the stove, reduce it until half the liquid has evaporated and the juice is concentrated. Use this concentrated juice in the recipe. You may have to add a little more water to the dough to achieve the proper consistency, because concentrated juice is thicker than normal.

- If using spices or seeds in pasta dough, be sure they are crushed or ground well enough so they won't tear the dough when it is rolled out. Use a mortar and pestle, coffee grinder (see page 71), or mini-chopper to render them as fine as coarsely ground pepper.

Method One

To make pasta dough in a food processor: This is the easiest way to make pasta dough, and my preferred method. Fit the food processor with the metal blade. Add the dry ingredients and pulse to combine. With the machine running, gradually pour the liquid (or combined liquids) through the feed tube. Process until the dough comes together into a rough ball (there may be a few stray scraps of dough on the bottom of the bowl), about 1 minute. Check the consistency of the dough. If it is too soft and very sticky, add a tablespoon or so more flour. If it is crumbly and dry, add a tablespoon of water. Process the dough for about 30 seconds and check again. When the dough is the proper consistency, knead it by processing for 1 minute. Gather up the dough and any scraps into a ball and knead it on a lightly floured work surface for a minute. This brief kneading by hand gives you a final consistency check. You may roll out the dough immediately, or cover it with plastic wrap and let it rest for 20 minutes.

Method Two

To make pasta dough in a heavy-duty electric mixer: Place the dry ingredients in the mixer bowl and make a well in the center. Add the liquid (or combined liquids) to the well. Attach the bowl to the mixer. Using the paddle blade, mix on medium speed just until the dough gathers into rough clumps. Remove the paddle, and gather the dough into a ball. Attach the dough hook, spear the dough onto the dough hook, and knead on medium speed until firm and supple (adding more flour or water, if needed), about 5 minutes. Transfer the dough to a lightly floured work surface and knead briefly to check the texture. Form the dough into a ball, cover with plastic wrap, and let rest at room temperature for 20 minutes.

Method Three

To make pasta dough in a bowl: Mix the dry ingredients in a medium bowl and make a well in the center. Pour the liquid (or combined liquids) into the well. Mix well to form a firm, slightly sticky dough, adding additional flour or water if needed. Gather up the dough into a ball. Knead on a lightly floured work surface until smooth and supple, at least 5 minutes. When the dough is ready, it will bounce back when pressed lightly with a fingertip. Form the dough into a ball, wrap in plastic wrap, and let rest for 20 minutes at room temperature before rolling out.

Method Four

To make pasta dough on a table or work surface: This method is much easier than it sounds, and lots of fun. Put the dry ingredients in a mound on a clean table or work surface, stir to combine, and make a well in the center. Pour the liquid (or combined liquids) into the well. Using a fork, stir the liquid(s) in a circular pattern, gradually making the circle bigger to incorporate more and more of the flour until the mixture forms a firm, slightly sticky dough. Add more flour or water if needed. Gather up the dough into a ball and scrape the work surface clean. Dust the work surface with more flour and knead the dough until smooth and supple, at least 5 minutes. When the dough is ready, it will bounce back when pressed lightly with a fingertip. Form the dough into a ball, wrap it in plastic wrap, and let rest for 20 minutes at room temperature before rolling out.

With practice, you can learn to make pasta dough as my Italian friends do—without measuring. They dump a pile of flour on the table, make a well, and add one egg for every estimated cup of flour. Next, they stir in enough liquid into the well to get the proper consistency and then gather the dough into a ball. The remaining flour is sifted to remove any moist lumps and saved for the next batch of pasta (which, in Italy, could be in a few hours).

ROLLING OUT THE DOUGH

There are two time-tested methods of hand-rolling pasta dough. The low-tech version is with a rolling pin. The mid-tech version is with a hand-cranked pasta machine. (The high-tech version is to leave it to the electric pasta machine, described in the next chapter.)

To roll out pasta dough with a rolling pin: This may sound daunting, but once you get the hang of it, you will be surprised at how quickly it goes. For best results, use a long, thick French-style rolling pin (about twenty inches long, with a diameter of one and three quarter inches), not an American ball bearing pin. This method works for flat noodles and for pasta for stuffing.

Cut the dough into six wedges. Work with one portion at a time, keeping the remaining dough well covered with plastic wrap. Dust the work surface and the rolling pin lightly with flour. Knead the pasta dough into a small, thick oblong. Throughout the whole procedure, think of stretching the dough, not just rolling it. Applying pressure, roll and stretch the dough into a 12-inch-long oblong. With the fingertips of one hand, hold the end of the oblong nearest you, and place the rolling pin on the pasta just above your fingertips. With your other hand, use pressure to roll the rolling pin away from you, stretching the dough as you do so. Flip the dough over, and rotate from top to bottom. Repeat the stretching procedure. Continue stretching and flipping the dough until it is about 24 inches long, and about 1/16 inch thick; stretch the dough as thin as possible without tearing, since it will retract slightly upon standing. (To continue see Drying the Dough below.)

To roll out pasta dough with a hand-cranked pasta machine: These recipes were tested on an Italian-made Atlas (or Marcato) brand pasta machine. Hand-cranked machines, which work on a theory similar to the old wringer washing machines, are relatively inexpensive. (Some have separate electric motor attachments for those who don't wish to use old-fashioned elbow grease to crank the machine.) Crank machines have two parallel rollers that can be adjusted to varying widths for kneading and stretching the dough. These machines are equipped with two different cutting rollers to cut pasta into fettuccine or linguine. Attachments are available for other widths and shapes (such as pappardelle or even ravioli), but for three-dimensional shapes, you may want to use an electric pasta machine or the new hand-cranked extruder machine described on page 33.

Cut the dough into six wedges. Work with only one piece at a time, and keep the remainder well covered with plastic wrap. Attach the pasta machine to the work surface. Place about half a cup of all-purpose flour on a baking sheet near the machine.

Form one portion of the dough into a thick oblong. Adjust the rollers to their widest setting (Number 1 on most machines) and insert the crank into the roller "keyhole." To knead the dough, fold the dough over into thirds and dip into the flour, coating on both sides. Crank the rollers and run the dough through the machine. If the dough has not rested long enough, or is too dry, it may crack slightly. Continue folding and rolling until the dough comes together, usually after five or six passes. If the dough seems too sticky, flour both sides before passing it through the rollers again. (Simply dip the dough in the flour on the baking sheet.) Some doughs take longer to knead and require more flour than others. Then knead the dough, without folding it, until smooth, five to ten passes.

Adjust the rollers to the next setting. Fold the dough into thirds again, flour both sides, and pass it through the rollers again. Continue folding and rolling for four more passes. Adjust the rollers to the next setting.

Fold the dough into thirds, flour, and roll again. Put the dough through the rollers for three more passes. By now the dough is transformed into a very smooth sheet of pasta.

Adjust the rollers to the next setting. Sprinkle the the pasta sheet well with flour, or drag it lightly through the flour on the baking sheet. Without folding into thirds, pass the sheet through the roller twice. (The dough will be quite long and thin. If the pasta is too long to handle, cut it in half crosswise with a sharp knife.) Adjust the roller to the next setting (Number 5), sprinkle well with flour, and roll a final time. If the dough sticks to itself as it comes out of the machine, fold it into a thick rectangle and re-roll, starting at the third setting and being sure to flour it well, especially as it is rolled into the thinner sheets. The dough should be about $\frac{1}{16}$ inch thick, which usually is accomplished with the second-to-the-last setting on the machine. If the dough is rolled thinner, it will tear easily and be too thin to hold together when cooked. I rarely use the Number Six or Seven settings. (To continue, see Drying the Dough below.)

DRYING THE DOUGH

As each sheet of dough is formed, transfer it to an area to dry before cutting it into shapes. I like to drape my pasta sheets over straight-backed chairs. Other cooks prop a broomstick between two chairs and drape the pasta over it. If you have lots of room, you can lay the pasta flat on a table covered with a well-floured tablecloth or kitchen towels. In any case, change the position of the pasta occasionally (flip if laid flat) to ensure even drying.

The exact length of drying time is difficult to estimate. Obviously, pasta dries more quickly on warm, dry days than on cold, wet ones. The pasta should be slightly moist to the touch, supple enough to roll without cracking, and almost leathery. This can take anywhere from twenty minutes to one hour. If the dough is too moist, it will stick to itself during cutting. If too dry, it will crack.

CUTTING THE DOUGH

To cut the dough by hand: Cut each pasta sheet crosswise in half (unless you cut it into smaller portions while rolling it). Starting at a short end, roll up one pasta sheet into a short cylinder. Using a sharp knife, cut across the cylinder into $\frac{1}{4}$-inch-thick strips for fettuccine or about $\frac{1}{8}$ inch thick for linguine. Unfurl the strips onto a lightly floured baking sheet. Continue with the remaining pasta sheets.

To cut the dough with a hand-cranked pasta machine: Place the crank into the "keyhole" next to the width you desire, either fettuccine or linguine. Crank each pasta sheet through the machine to cut. Gather up the strips and transfer to a lightly floured baking sheet.

To be sure that the cut pasta doesn't stick to itself, sprinkle it with a dusting of flour, semolina, or cornmeal. Toss the pasta with the flour or cornmeal between your fingers until well coated. (The flour or cornmeal will wash off during boiling.)

The pasta can be cooked immediately. However, you will have increased control over the cooking procedure if you let it dry, turning occasionally, for a couple of hours before using. If you do proceed as soon as the pasta is cut, remember that very fresh pasta cooks very quickly. (See How to Cook and Serve Pasta, page 14. The water may not even have come back to a boil by the time the pasta is overcooked.) To store uncooked pasta, transfer it to a plastic bag and refrigerate for up to two days or freeze for up to one month.

HANDMADE PASTA SHAPES—A NEW DEVELOPMENT

Until very recently, three-dimensional pasta shapes had to be made in an electric pasta machine. Now, Atlas (Marcato) has a reasonably priced hand-cranked extrusion machine that produces shapes such as ribbed tubular pasta in three widths, bucatini, and rotini. (Use the regular hand-cranked machine to create the flat ribbon shapes like fettuccine, linguine, and lasagne.) Any of these handmade dough recipes will work in this new hand-cranked machine, but I find they work best if you add a tablespoon of oil to the dough when mixing it. This softens the dough slightly. Also, do not try a 100 percent semolina dough in this machine; it is a little too firm to extrude without effort.

CLEANING THE PASTA MACHINE

All the pasta machine needs in a dusting off with a dry pastry brush. Never immerse it in water. If you detect scraps of pasta dough in the cutting rollers, run a paper towel through the rollers to clean them.

CLASSIC EGG PASTA

Hand Method

MAKES ABOUT 1 POUND DOUGH

————

The wheat-and-egg noodle is the workhorse of the pasta family. This tender pasta is created from a simple blend of unbleached wheat flour, eggs (or in our case, cholesterol-free liquid egg substitute or egg whites), and just enough water to convince the dough to hold together. This is a good pasta for beginners, as it can be rolled out by hand or by crank machine. Cut into thin noodles, it can be an Italian linguine to be sauced and savored—or a Chinese egg noodle to turn into a sizzling stir-fry.

————

2 cups unbleached all-purpose flour
½ cup liquid egg substitute or 4 large egg whites
2 to 4 tablespoons water

————

Using one of the four methods described on pages 29 to 30, make the pasta dough. Roll out, dry, and cut the dough as directed on pages 30 to 33.

SUGGESTED RECIPES

Lean Pesto Linguine, Faux Fettuccine Alfredo, Better-for-You Fettuccine Bolognese, Thai Chicken-Basil Sauce with Linguine, Vegetable and Noodle Stir-Fry, Egg Noodles with Peking Turkey and Vegetable Sauce, Scallops in Rosemary-Vermouth Sauce on Linguine, Fettuccine with Arugula Pesto, Wild Mushroom Ragout Pasta

---

NUTRITIONAL ANALYSIS PER SERVING (BASED ON 8 SERVINGS)

CALORIES: 127 (17 percent from protein, 77 percent from carbohydrates, 6 percent from fat) • PROTEIN: 5 grams • CARBOHYDRATE: 24 grams • FAT: 1 gram • CHOLESTEROL: 0 milligrams • SODIUM: 28 milligrams

TRADITIONAL SEMOLINA AND EGG PASTA

Hand Method

MAKES ABOUT 1 POUND DOUGH

Semolina gives this pasta character and a golden hue. This is the best semolina-based dough to make if you are rolling out the pasta with a pin. If you are going to roll out the dough in a hand-cranked machine, use all semolina instead of a mix of semolina and all-purpose flour. Any Italian-style sauce will taste exquisite with this pasta.

1 cup unbleached all-purpose flour
1 cup durum semolina (also called pasta flour)
½ cup liquid egg substitute or 4 large egg whites
1 to 2 tablespoons water, if needed

Using one of the four methods described on pages 29 to 30, make the pasta dough. Roll out, dry, and cut the dough as directed on pages 30 to 33.

SUGGESTED RECIPES

Coal Miner's Light Fettuccine, Herbed Marinara Sauce with Linguine, Better-for-You Fettuccine Bolognese, San Francisco Cio-Pasta, Pasta with Mushroom Marsala

NUTRITIONAL ANALYSIS PER SERVING (BASED ON 8 SERVINGS)

CALORIES: 145 (17 percent from protein, 77 percent from carbohydrate, 6 percent from fat) • PROTEIN: 6 grams • CARBOHYDRATE: 27 grams • FAT: 1 gram • CHOLESTEROL: 0 milligrams • SODIUM: 28 milligrams

SEMOLINA PASTA CLASSICA

Hand Method

MAKES ABOUT 1 POUND DOUGH

Pasta Italian-style. Semolina and water, that's it—creating a firm-textured pasta that will stand up to sturdy sauces. The dough will seem slightly crumbly the first few times you pass it through the rollers for kneading, but it will smooth out as it is worked. I do not recommend rolling this dough out with a rolling pin. If you are a novice to pasta making, start with Traditional Semolina and Egg Pasta (page 35).

----

2 cups durum semolina (also called pasta flour)
Approximately ½ cup water

Using one of the four methods described on pages 29 to 30, make the pasta dough. Roll out, dry, and cut the dough as directed on pages 30 to 33.

SUGGESTED RECIPES

Lean Pesto Linguine, Faux Fettuccine Alfredo, Herbed
Marinara Sauce with Linguine, Better-for-You Fettuccine
Bolognese

NUTRITIONAL ANALYSIS PER SERVING (BASED ON 8 SERVINGS)

CALORIES: 150 (14 percent from protein, 83 percent from carbohydrate, 3 percent from fat) • PROTEIN: 5 grams • CARBOHYDRATE: 31 grams • FAT: less than 1 gram • CHOLESTEROL: 0 milligrams • SODIUM: 1 milligram

CHINESE WATER NOODLE DOUGH

Hand Method

MAKES ABOUT 1 POUND DOUGH

China's basic pasta dough, it can be cut into thin noodles for soups and stir-fries.

---

2 cups unbleached all-purpose flour
½ cup warm water

Using one of the four methods described on pages 29 to 30, make the pasta dough. Roll out, dry, and cut the dough as directed on pages 30 to 33.

SUGGESTED RECIPES

Thai Chicken-Basil Sauce with Linguine, Vegetable and Noodle Stir-Fry

---

NUTRITIONAL ANALYSIS PER SERVING (BASED ON 8 SERVINGS)
CALORIES: 113 (12 percent from protein, 86 percent from carbohydrate, 2 percent from fat) • PROTEIN: less than 1 gram • CARBOHYDRATE: 3 grams • FAT: less than 1 gram • CHOLESTEROL: 0 milligrams • SODIUM: 1 milligram

TOMATO BLUSH PASTA

Hand Method

MAKES ABOUT 1 POUND DOUGH

This dough is worth making for its subtle pastel pink shade, but allow your sauce to provide the tomato flavor—you can barely taste it in the pasta itself.

¼ cup tomato paste
3 tablespoons water, or more if needed
2 cups unbleached all-purpose flour
6 tablespoons liquid egg substitute or 3 large egg whites

In a glass measuring cup, whisk the tomato paste in the water until dissolved. Using one of the four methods described on pages 29 to 30, make the pasta dough. Roll out, dry, and cut the dough as directed on pages 30 to 33.

Variation

TOMATO BLUSH SEMOLINA PASTA

Substitute 1 cup durum semolina (pasta flour) for 1 cup of the all-purpose flour.

SUGGESTED RECIPE

Linguine with Chunky Roasted Pepper Cream

NUTRITIONAL ANALYSIS PER SERVING (BASED ON 8 SERVINGS)

CALORIES: 131 (15 percent from protein, 79 percent from carbohydrate, 5 percent from fat) • PROTEIN: 5 grams • CARBOHYDRATE: 25 grams • FAT: 1 gram • CHOLESTEROL: less than 1 milligram • SODIUM: 86 milligrams

EMERALD SPINACH PASTA

Hand Method

MAKES ABOUT 1 POUND DOUGH

Emerald Spinach Pasta has a deep forest-green color that provides a touch of drama in the simplest dish. The flavor is remarkably mild, though, and goes nicely with a variety of sauces.

---

1 10-ounce package frozen chopped spinach, defrosted and
squeezed dry
¼ cup liquid egg substitute or 2 large egg whites
5 tablespoons water, or more if needed
2 cups unbleached all-purpose flour

In a small bowl, combine the spinach, liquid egg substitute and water. Using one of the four methods described on pages 000 to 000, make the pasta dough, adding water as needed. (The food processor method works best, as the blade will continue to mince the spinach as the dough mixes.) Roll out, dry, and cut the dough as directed on pages 30 to 33.

(continued)

Variation

EMERALD SPINACH SEMOLINA PASTA

Substitute 1 cup durum semolina (pasta flour) for 1 cup of the all-purpose flour.

❖
SUGGESTED RECIPES

Faux Fettuccine Alfredo, Pasta with Mushroom Marsala,
Shellfish and Mushroom Lasagne

NUTRITIONAL ANALYSIS PER SERVING (BASED ON 8 SERVINGS)
CALORIES: 127 (16 percent from protein, 80 percent from carbohydrate, 4 percent from fat) •
PROTEIN: 5 grams • CARBOHYDRATE: 25 grams • FAT: 1 gram • CHOLESTEROL: 0 milligrams •
SODIUM: 35 milligrams

BRIGHT BEET PASTA
Hand Method

MAKES ABOUT 1 POUND DOUGH

When a friend rolled out this vibrantly garnet-colored pasta, she remarked that it looked and felt like a luxurious silk scarf. You'll gather compliments for its taste as well as its looks. Make the pasta as soon as you've juiced the beets—the juice loses its color if allowed to stand.

½ cup fresh beet juice (from about 8 ounces beets)
1 teaspoon canola or olive oil
2 cups unbleached all-purpose flour
Water, if needed

In a glass measuring cup, combine the beet juice and oil. Using one of the four methods described on pages 29 to 30, make the pasta dough, adding water if needed. Roll out, dry, and cut the dough as directed on pages 30 to 33.

Variation

BRIGHT BEET SEMOLINA PASTA

Substitute 1 cup durum semolina (pasta flour) for 1 cup of the all-purpose flour.

SUGGESTED RECIPE

Springtime Sugar Snap and Herb Pasta

NUTRITIONAL ANALYSIS PER SERVING (BASED ON 8 SERVINGS)

CALORIES: 123 (11 percent from protein, 82 percent from carbohydrate, 7 percent from fat) • PROTEIN: 3 grams • CARBOHYDRATE: 25 grams • FAT: 1 gram • CHOLESTEROL: 0 milligrams • SODIUM: 7 milligrams

GOLDEN CARROT PASTA

Hand Method

MAKES ABOUT 1 POUND DOUGH

Carrot juice colors this pasta a bright harvest orange, and supplies a slightly sweet note that goes well with fresh vegetable sauces. Mix this with Bright Beet Pasta (page 40) and Emerald Spinach Pasta (page 39) for a sensational, tricolor effect.

1 *cup unbleached all-purpose flour*
1 *cup durum semolina (also called pasta flour)*
⅔ cup fresh carrot juice (from 5 medium carrots)
1 *teaspoon canola or olive oil*
Water, if needed

In a glass measuring cup, combine the carrot juice and oil. Using one of the four methods described on pages 29 to 30, make the pasta dough, adding water if needed. Roll out, dry, and cut the dough as directed on pages 30 to 33.

Variation

CARROT-GINGER PASTA

Juice a 3-ounce piece of ginger along with the carrots.

Variation

CARROT-ORANGE PASTA

Mix the zest of 2 large oranges with the canola oil to make a paste, and mix into the carrot juice. Or, mix in ¼ teaspoon of orange-flavored oil (see page 19).

SUGGESTED RECIPES

Linguine with Chunky Roasted Pepper Cream, Springtime Sugar Snap and Herb Pasta

---

NUTRITIONAL ANALYSIS PER SERVING (BASED ON 8 SERVINGS)

CALORIES: 145 (12 percent from protein, 81 percent from carbohydrate, 6 percent from fat) • PROTEIN: 4 grams • CARBOHYDRATE: 29 grams • FAT: 1 gram • CHOLESTEROL: 0 milligrams • SODIUM: 6 milligrams

MINTED ZUCCHINI PASTA

Hand Method

A delicate pale green, this pasta is perfect with vividly seasoned tomato sauces. While I find mint highly compatible with tomatoes, you may wish to use basil or oregano.

½ cup fresh zucchini juice (from 3 medium zucchini)
1 tablespoon dried mint, basil, or oregano
2 cups unbleached all-purpose flour
Water, if needed

In a glass measuring cup, combine the zucchini juice and mint. Using one of the four methods described on pages 29 to 30, make the pasta dough, adding water if needed. Roll out, dry, and cut the dough as directed on pages 30 to 33.

Variation

MINTED ZUCCHINI SEMOLINA PASTA

Substitute 1 cup durum semolina (pasta flour) for 1 cup of the all-purpose flour.

SUGGESTED RECIPE

Lean Pesto Linguine

NUTRITIONAL ANALYSIS PER SERVING (BASED ON 8 SERVINGS)

CALORIES: 119 (12 percent from protein, 86 percent from carbohydrate, 3 percent from fat) • PROTEIN: 3 grams • CARBOHYDRATE: 25 grams • FAT: less than 1 gram • CHOLESTEROL: 0 milligrams • SODIUM: 1 milligram

SUN-DRIED TOMATO AND GARLIC PASTA

Hand Method

MAKES ABOUT 1 POUND DOUGH

———

This has a slightly deeper color and flavor than the Tomato Blush Pasta (page 38) and is freckled with specks of sun-dried tomatoes.

———

3 ounces loose-packed sun-dried tomatoes, soaked and drained (see page 23)
¼ cup liquid egg substitute or 2 large egg whites
3 tablespoons water, plus more as needed
2 garlic cloves
1 cup unbleached all-purpose flour
1 cup durum semolina (also called pasta flour)

———

In a blender, process the soaked sun-dried tomatoes, liquid egg substitute, 3 tablespoons water, and garlic cloves until smooth. Using one of the four methods described on pages 29 to 30, make the pasta dough, adding water if needed. Roll out, dry, and cut the dough as directed on pages 30 to 33.

SUGGESTED RECIPES

Faux Fettuccine Alfredo,
Sicilian Tuna and Tomato Pasta

NUTRITIONAL ANALYSIS PER SERVING (BASED ON 8 SERVINGS)
CALORIES: 169 (15 percent from protein, 81 percent from carbohydrate, 4 percent from fat) • PROTEIN: 6 grams • CARBOHYDRATE: 35 grams • FAT: 1 gram • CHOLESTEROL: less than 1 milligram • SODIUM: 27 milligrams

PESTO PASTA

Hand Method

MAKES ABOUT 1 POUND DOUGH

The pesto flavor is tangible but not overwhelming, and the color is a lovely shade of green, making this a versatile pasta suitable for many dishes. For a more intense basil flavor, add a quarter teaspoon basil-flavored oil (see page 19) to the egg substitute.

½ cup Lean Pesto (page 88)
¼ cup liquid egg substitute or 2 large egg whites
2 cups unbleached all-purpose flour
Water, as needed

In a medium bowl, whisk the pesto and egg substitute until well blended. Using one of the four methods described on pages 29 to 30, make the pasta dough, adding water if needed. Roll out, dry, and cut the dough as directed on pages 30 to 33.

Variation

PESTO SEMOLINA PASTA

Substitute 1 cup durum semolina (pasta flour) for 1 cup of the all-purpose flour.

SUGGESTED RECIPES

Better-for-You Fettuccine Bolognese, San Francisco Cio-
Pasta, Sautéed Scallops with Confetti Vegetables and
Linguine

NUTRITIONAL ANALYSIS PER SERVING (BASED ON 8 SERVINGS)

CALORIES: 131 (16 percent from protein, 76 percent from carbohydrate, 9 percent from fat) •
PROTEIN: 5 grams • CARBOHYDRATE: 24 grams • FAT: 1 gram • CHOLESTEROL: 2 milligrams •
SODIUM: 99 milligrams

WILD MUSHROOM PASTA

Hand Method

MAKES ABOUT 1 POUND DOUGH

Dried porcini mushrooms give real Italian authority to this pasta, but other dried mushrooms, according to budget and availability, are also acceptable. This is not an everyday pasta, and should be made only for special occasions—or to soothe spirits when a treat is needed.

------

1 ounce (about 1 cup) dried wild mushrooms (porcini, chanterelles, cèpes, or morels)
1 cup unbleached all-purpose flour
1 cup durum semolina (also called pasta flour)
½ cup liquid egg substitute or 4 large egg whites
6 to 8 tablespoons water

Using a pastry brush, carefully brush the dried mushrooms to remove as much grit as possible. In a coffee grinder or blender, process the dried mushrooms to a fine powder. Using one of the four methods described on pages 29 to 30, make the pasta dough. Roll out, dry, and cut the dough as directed on pages 30 to 33.

SUGGESTED RECIPES

Pasta with Mushroom Marsala, Vegetarian Lasagne, Fettuccine with Sautéed Radicchio and Caramelized Onions, Asparagus and Ricotta Pasta, Wild Mushroom Ragout Pasta

NUTRITIONAL ANALYSIS PER SERVING (BASED ON 8 SERVINGS)

CALORIES: 156 (17 percent from protein, 78 percent from carbohydrate, 5 percent from fat) • PROTEIN: 6 grams • CARBOHYDRATE: 30 grams • FAT: 1 gram • CHOLESTEROL: less than 1 milligram • SODIUM: 29 milligrams

LEMON-PARSLEY PASTA

Hand Method

MAKES ABOUT 1 POUND DOUGH

——

Seafood is a natural match for this brightly flavored pasta. If available, substitute ½ teaspoon lemon-flavored oil (see page 19) for the zest and oil.

——

Grated zest of 3 lemons
1 teaspoon canola or olive oil
½ cup fresh lemon juice
2 cups unbleached all-purpose flour
⅓ cup chopped fresh parsley
1 teaspoon salt
Water, if needed

——

In a small bowl, mix the lemon zest and oil to a paste. Add to the lemon juice. Using one of the four methods described on pages 29 to 30, make the pasta dough. Roll out, dry, and cut the dough as directed on pages 30 to 33.

SUGGESTED RECIPES

San Francisco Cio-Pasta, Scallops in Rosemary-Vermouth Sauce on Linguine, Sautéed Scallops with Confetti Vegetables and Linguine, Shellfish and Mushroom Lasagne

---

NUTRITIONAL ANALYSIS PER SERVING (BASED ON 8 SERVINGS)

CALORIES: 124 (11 percent from protein, 83 percent from carbohydrate, 7 percent from fat) •
PROTEIN: 3 grams • CARBOHYDRATE: 26 grams • FAT: 1 gram • CHOLESTEROL: 0 milligrams •
SODIUM: 268 milligrams

LIME-PEPPER PASTA

Hand Method

MAKES ABOUT I POUND DOUGH

Lime and corn complement each other in this Mexican-inspired pasta. If available, substitute ½ teaspoon lime-flavored oil (see page 19) for the zest.

Grated zest of 3 limes
1 teaspoon canola or olive oil
½ cup fresh lime juice
1¾ cups unbleached all-purpose flour
¼ cup yellow cornmeal
1 teaspoon salt
1 tablespoon coarsely cracked black pepper
Water, if needed

In a small bowl, mix the lime zest and oil to a paste. Add to the lime juice. Using one of the four methods described on pages 29 to 30, make the pasta dough. Roll out, dry, and cut the dough as directed on pages 30 to 33.

SUGGESTED RECIPES

Thai Chicken-Basil Sauce with Linguine,
Spicy Cajun Shrimp on Linguine

NUTRITIONAL ANALYSIS PER SEVING (BASED ON 8 SERVINGS)

CALORIES: 125 (10 percent from protein, 82 percent from carbohydrate, 7 percent from fat) • PROTEIN: 3 grams • CARBOHYDRATE: 26 grams • FAT: 1 gram • CHOLESTEROL: 0 milligrams • SODIUM: 269 milligrams

CURRY PASTA

Hand Method

MAKES ABOUT 1 POUND DOUGH

Curry powder contributes both exotic flavor and a bright yellow hue to this pasta. Search out curry powders marked "Madras-style" for a spice blend that is reliable.

¼ cup plain nonfat yogurt
¼ cup water, or more if needed
2 cups unbleached all-purpose flour
2 tablespoons curry powder, preferably Madras-style

In a small bowl, whisk together the yogurt and ¼ cup water. Using one of the four methods described on pages 29 to 30, make the pasta dough. Roll out, dry, and cut the dough as directed on pages 30 to 33.

SUGGESTED RECIPE

Fettuccine with Madras Chicken Yogurt Sauce

NUTRITIONAL ANALYSIS PER SERVING (BASED ON 8 SERVINGS)

CALORIES: 122 (13 percent from protein, 83 percent from carbohydrate, 4 percent from fat) • PROTEIN: 4 grams • CARBOHYDRATE: 25 grams • FAT: 1 gram • CHOLESTEROL: less than 1 milligram • SODIUM: 7 milligrams

MEXICAN CHILI AND CILANTRO PASTA

Hand Method

MAKES ABOUT 1 POUND DOUGH

W hen chosing a chili powder, most pasta makers will prefer the familiar somewhat mild blend that that includes ground chiles, cumin, and other spices. (It is called "chili" powder, with an "i," because it is used to season "chili.") There is also ground chile powder (with an "e"), which is 100 percent powdered dried hot chile peppers without added spices. Either will work in this pasta—with different levels of hotness, of course.

¼ cup liquid egg substitute or 2 large egg whites
2 tablespoons tomato paste
2 tablespoons water, plus more as needed
1¾ cups unbleached all-purpose flour
¼ cup yellow cornmeal
⅓ cup chopped fresh cilantro
2 tablespoons chili powder or pure ground chile powder

In a small bowl, whisk together the egg substitute, tomato paste, and 2 tablespoons water. Using one of the four methods described on pages 29 to 30, make the pasta dough. Roll out, dry, and cut the dough as directed on pages 30 to 33.

(continued)

SUGGESTED RECIPE

Shrimp with Tomatoes, Corn, and Black Beans
on Linguine

NUTRITIONAL ANALYSIS PER SERVING (BASED ON 8 SERVINGS)

CALORIES: 130 (14 percent from protein, 79 percent from carbohydrate, 7 percent from fat) •
PROTEIN: 4 grams • CARBOHYDRATE: 26 grams • FAT: 1 gram • CHOLESTEROL: 0 milligrams •
SODIUM: 68 milligrams

SPICY CAJUN PASTA

Hand Method

———

Cajun seasoning blends are available on every supermarket spice shelf. If you would like to make your own, mix one tablespoon sweet or hot Hungarian paprika with one teaspoon dried thyme, one teaspoon dried basil, one teaspoon dried oregano, one half teaspoon onion powder, one half teaspoon garlic powder, and one quarter teaspoon cayenne pepper.

———

¼ cup liquid egg substitute or 2 large egg whites
¼ cup tomato-vegetable juice blend, plus more if needed
1¾ cups unbleached all-purpose flour
¼ cup yellow cornmeal
2 tablespoons Cajun seasoning blend

———

In a small bowl, whisk together the egg substitute and juice. Using one of the four methods described on pages 29 to 30, make the pasta dough, adding more juice if needed. Roll out, dry, and cut the dough as directed on pages 30 to 33.

SUGGESTED RECIPE

Spicy Cajun Shrimp on Linguine

NUTRITIONAL ANALYSIS PER SERVING (BASED ON 8 SERVINGS)

CALORIES: 126 (14 percent from protein, 80 percent from carbohydrate, 6 percent from fat) • PROTEIN: 4 grams • CARBOHYDRATE: 25 grams • FAT: 1 gram • CHOLESTEROL: 0 milligrams • SODIUM: 44 milligrams

MARYLAND SPICE BOX PASTA

Hand Method

MAKES ABOUT 1 POUND DOUGH

———

A Chesapeake Bay kitchen just wouldn't be authentic without a yellow can of Old Bay Seasoning, that wonderful mix of myriad spices and herbs. It adds zest to the Fettuccine with Crab Hash on page 145 and to this pasta, but you will find many other uses for it; I love it in coleslaw and (when I am splurging on fat calories) in the coating for fried chicken.

———

2 cups unbleached all-purpose flour
3 tablespoons Old Bay Seasoning
½ cup water
1 teaspoon canola oil

———

Using one of the four methods described on pages 29 to 30, make the pasta dough. Roll out, dry, and cut the dough as directed on pages 30 to 33.

SUGGESTED RECIPE

Fettuccine with Crab Hash

NUTRITIONAL ANALYSIS PER SERVING (BASED ON 8 SERVINGS)

CALORIES: 124 (11 percent from protein, 81 percent from carbohydrate, 8 percent from fat) • PROTEIN: 3 grams • CARBOHYDRATE: 25 grams • FAT: 1 gram • CHOLESTEROL: 0 milligrams • SODIUM: 269 milligrams

GINGER-CITRUS PASTA

Hand Method

MAKES ABOUT 1 POUND DOUGH

I usually prefer to use fresh ginger, but this recipe uses the ground variety for ease in preparation.

---

1 *large orange*
1 *large lemon*
1 *teaspoon canola oil*
2 *cups unbleached all-purpose flour*
1 *tablespoon plus 1½ teaspoons ground ginger*
Water, if needed

---

1. Using a hand grater, remove the zest from the orange and lemon. In a small bowl, mix the zests with the oil to form a paste.

2. Squeeze the juices from the fruits and measure. You should have ½ cup combined juices; add more juice or water if necessary. Stir the juices into the zest paste. Using one of the four methods described on pages 29 to 30, make the pasta dough, adding water if needed. Roll out, dry, and cut the dough as directed on pages 30 to 33.

SUGGESTED RECIPES

Thai Chicken-Basil Sauce with Linguine, Sautéed Scallops with Confetti Vegetables and Linguine

---

NUTRITIONAL ANALYSIS PER SERVING (BASED ON 8 SERVINGS)

CALORIES: 129 (11 percent from protein, 83 percent from carbohydrate, 7 percent from fat) • PROTEIN: 3 grams • CARBOHYDRATE: 27 grams • FAT: 1 gram • CHOLESTEROL: 0 milligrams • SODIUM: 1 milligram

SCALLION PANCAKE PASTA

Hand Method

MAKES ABOUT 1 POUND DOUGH

———

Here I've taken a favorite Chinese nibble and transformed it into pasta. If you wish, use hot sesame oil instead of the mild dark variety. Be sure to include the cilantro stems—they add lots of flavor to the dough.

———

½ cup chopped scallions (2 scallions)
½ cup chopped fresh cilantro, leaves and stems
2 teaspoons dark Asian sesame oil
¼ cup water, plus more as needed
2 cups unbleached all-purpose flour

———

In a blender, process the scallions, cilantro leaves and stems, oil, and ¼ cup of the water until smooth, 1 minute or longer. Using one of the four methods described on pages 29 to 30, make the pasta dough. Roll out, dry, and cut the dough as directed on pages 30 to 33.

SUGGESTED RECIPE

Egg Noodles with Peking Turkey and Vegetable Sauce

NUTRITIONAL ANALYSIS PER SERVING (BASED ON 8 SERVINGS)

CALORIES: 124 (11 percent from protein, 79 percent from carbohydrate, 11 percent from fat) •
PROTEIN: 3 grams • CARBOHYDRATE: 24 grams • FAT: 1 gram • CHOLESTEROL: 0 milligrams •
SODIUM: 1 milligram

FRESH GARDEN HERB PASTA

Hand Method

MAKES ABOUT 1 POUND DOUGH

You can use three quarters of a cup of any chopped herbs you prefer—dill, tarragon, oregano, marjoram, or cilantro, or a mix—from whatever your garden or greengrocer offers. This is a favorite blend of mine, featuring my own garden's bounty.

½ cup packed chopped fresh basil leaves
⅓ cup water, or more if needed
¼ cup chopped fresh parsley
1 tablespoon chopped fresh chives
2 garlic cloves, crushed
1 teaspoon canola or olive oil
1 cup unbleached all-purpose flour
1 cup durum semolina (also called pasta flour)

In a blender, process the basil, ⅓ cup water, parsley, chives, garlic, and oil until smooth, 1 minute or longer. Using one of the four methods described on pages 29 to 30, make the pasta dough, adding water if needed. Roll out, dry, and cut the dough as directed on pages 30 to 33.

SUGGESTED RECIPES

Scallops in Rosemary-Vermouth Sauce on Linguine,
Shellfish and Mushroom Lasagne

NUTRITIONAL ANALYSIS PER SERVING (BASED ON 8 SERVINGS)

CALORIES: 139 (13 percent from protein, 81 percent from carbohydrate, 6 percent from fat) • PROTEIN: 4 grams • CARBOHYDRATE: 26 grams • FAT: 1 gram • CHOLESTEROL: 0 milligrams • SODIUM: 2 milligrams

MIXED PEPPERCORN PASTA

Hand Method

MAKES ABOUT 1 POUND DOUGH

———

If your specialty food stores carry a blend of black, white, pink, and green peppercorns, use it. Otherwise, coarsely grind two tablespoons of whatever peppercorns you have on hand.

———

1 cup unbleached all-purpose flour
1 cup durum semolina (also called pasta flour)
2 tablespoons coarsely ground mixed peppercorns
½ cup liquid egg substitute or 4 large egg whites
Water, if needed

———

Using one of the four methods described on pages 29 to 30, make the pasta dough, adding water if needed. Roll out, dry, and cut the dough as directed on pages 30 to 33.

SUGGESTED RECIPES

Faux Fettuccine Alfredo, Coal Miner's Light Fettuccine,
Artichoke, Turkey Ham, and Sun-dried Tomato
Fettuccine, Pasta with Mushroom Marsala

NUTRITIONAL ANALYSIS PER SERVING (BASED ON 8 SERVINGS)

CALORIES: 149 (17 percent from protein, 77 percent from carbohydrate, 6 percent from fat) • PROTEIN: 6 grams • CARBOHYDRATE: 28 grams • FAT: 1 gram • CHOLESTEROL: less than 1 milligram • SODIUM: 29 milligrams

SAFFRON PASTA

Hand Method

MAKES ABOUT 1 POUND DOUGH

——

This maize-colored pasta always makes a highly favorable impression. For best flavor, buy high-quality Spanish saffron threads (not powder).

——

1 teaspoon crushed saffron threads (see above)
½ cup liquid egg substitute or 4 large egg whites
1 cup unbleached all-purpose flour
1 cup durum semolina (also called pasta flour)
Water, as needed

——

1. Toast the saffron in a dry nonstick skillet over medium-low heat, stirring constantly, until the threads are slightly brittle, 1 to 2 minutes. Cool, then crush in a mortar or between two large spoons. Stir into the egg substitute.

2. Using one of the four methods described on pages 29 to 30, make the pasta dough, adding water if needed. Roll out, dry, and cut the dough as directed on pages 30 to 33.

SUGGESTED RECIPES

Shrimp with Tomatoes, Corn, and Black Beans on
Linguine, Artichoke, Turkey Ham, and Sun-dried Tomato
Fettuccine, Linguine with Chunky Roasted Pepper Cream

NUTRITIONAL ANALYSIS PER SERVING (BASED ON 8 SERVINGS)

CALORIES: 145 (17 percent from protein, 77 percent from carbohydrate, 6 percent from fat) • PROTEIN: 6 grams • CARBOHYDRATE: 27 grams • FAT: 1 gram • CHOLESTEROL: less than 1 milligram • SODIUM: 28 milligrams

WHOLE WHEAT PASTA

Hand Method

MAKES ABOUT 1 POUND DOUGH

This makes a chewy, firm noodle that is wonderful in soups or with strongly flavored sauces. The best whole wheat flour can be found at your natural food store. Store all whole-grain flours in the refrigerator, as they spoil easily.

1 cup unbleached all-purpose flour
1 cup whole wheat flour
½ cup liquid egg substitute or 4 large egg whites
¼ cup water, plus more as needed

Using one of the four methods described on pages 29 to 30, make the pasta dough. Roll out, dry, and cut the dough as directed on pages 30 to 33.

Variation

TRITICALE PASTA

Substitute 1 cup triticale flour for the whole wheat.

Variation

KAMUT PASTA

Substitute 1 cup kamut flour for the whole wheat.

Variation

SPELT PASTA

This is the pasta to make for wheat-intolerant people. Substitute 2 cups spelt flour for the all-purpose and whole wheat flours.

SUGGESTED RECIPES

Lean Pesto Linguine, Garlic-Vegetable Soup with Whole Wheat Noodles, Fettuccine with Sautéed Radicchio and Caramelized Onions

NUTRITIONAL ANALYSIS PER SERVING (BASED ON 8 SERVINGS)

CALORIES: 121 (18 percent from protein, 75 percent from carbohydrate, 7 percent from fat) • PROTEIN: 6 grams • CARBOHYDRATE: 23 grams • FAT: 1 gram • CHOLESTEROL: less than 1 milligram • SODIUM: 29 milligrams

RYE PASTA

Hand Method

MAKES ABOUT I POUND DOUGH

———

Anyone who loves rye bread (count me in) will love this pasta and its pumpernickel variation (page 65) too. Don't be tempted to increase the amount of rye flour in the dough. Rye flour is very absorbent, and you'll end up with a sticky mess. One of my favorite ways to serve this is as a simple side dish: Simply toss the hot noodles with room temperature nonfat sour cream alternative, and sprinkle with chives and freshly ground pepper—that's it.

———

1 cup unbleached all-purpose flour
½ cup whole wheat flour
½ cup rye flour
½ cup liquid egg substitute or 4 large egg whites
2 to 4 tablespoons water

———

Using one of the four methods described on pages 29 to 30, make the pasta dough, adding water as needed. Roll out, dry, and cut the dough as directed on pages 30 to 33.

SUGGESTED RECIPE
Fettuccine with Sautéed Radicchio and Caramelized
Onions

NUTRITIONAL ANALYSIS PER SERVING (BASED ON 8 SERVINGS)

CALORIES: 118 (17 percent from protein, 76 percent from carbohydrate, 7 percent from fat) • PROTEIN: 5 grams • CARBOHYDRATE: 22 grams • FAT: 1 gram • CHOLESTEROL: less than 1 milligram • SODIUM: 29 milligrams

PUMPERNICKEL PASTA
Hand Method

MAKES ABOUT 1 POUND PASTA DOUGH

There is no such thing as a pumpernickel grain. Pumpernickel, the heartiest, darkest rye bread in the genre, is named after its originator. Some pumpernickels are flavored with onions and caraway; this pasta takes its call from those.

½ cup liquid egg substitute or 4 large egg whites
3 tablespoons nonfat sour cream alternative
2 teaspoons caraway seeds, ground
1 cup unbleached all-purpose flour
½ cup whole wheat flour
½ cup rye flour
1 tablespoon cocoa powder
1 teaspoon onion powder
½ teaspoon salt
Water, as needed

In a small bowl, whisk together the egg substitute, sour cream, and caraway seed. Using one of the four methods described on pages 29 to 30, make the pasta dough, adding water as needed. Roll out, dry, and cut the dough as directed on pages 30 to 33.

SUGGESTED RECIPE
Wild Mushroom Ragout Pasta

NUTRITIONAL ANALYSIS PER SERVING (BASED ON 8 SERVINGS)
CALORIES: 129 (19 percent from protein, 73 percent from carbohydrate, 8 percent from fat) • PROTEIN: 6 grams • CARBOHYDRATE: 24 grams • FAT: 1 gram • CHOLESTEROL: less than 1 milligram • SODIUM: 166 milligrams

MIXED GRAIN PASTA

Hand Method

MAKES ABOUT 1 POUND DOUGH

———

When I can't decide which whole-grain pasta to make, I make this distinctive dough, which uses wheat, rye, and corn.

———

1 ¼ cups unbleached all-purpose flour
⅔ cup whole wheat flour
3 tablespoons rye flour
2 tablespoons yellow cornmeal
½ cup liquid egg substitute or 4 large egg whites
3 to 4 tablespoons water

———

Using one of the four methods described on pages 29 to 30, make the pasta dough. Roll out, dry, and cut the dough as directed on pages 30 to 33.

SUGGESTED RECIPES

Garlic-Vegetable Soup with Whole Wheat Noodles,
Fettuccine with Sautéed Radicchio and Caramelized
Onions

NUTRITIONAL ANALYSIS PER SERVING (BASED ON 8 SERVINGS)

CALORIES: 133 (17 percent from protein, 76 percent from carbohydrate, 7 percent from fat) • PROTEIN: 6 grams • CARBOHYDRATE: 26 grams • FAT: 1 gram • CHOLESTEROL: less than 1 milligram • SODIUM: 29 milligrams

4

Pasta Presto:
Using an Electric
Pasta Extruder Machine

Versatility and fun are the primary reasons for using an electric pasta machine. The machines come with a collection of dies that allow the cook to create an assortment of pasta shapes at home. With them, you can make your own macaroni, rotini, and other twisty, curly, three-dimensional pastas that were once only available at the grocer's.

I prefer handmade pasta to the electric version. Nothing can match the texture of lovingly made hands-on pasta. It's a matter of personal preference and dexterity. But I know some of you own and love electric pasta machines—this chapter is for you.

Unlike bread machines, where the cook simply tosses in a few ingredients and turns on the switch, electric pasta machines are not "no-brainers." They operate as extruders: Dough is mixed in an inner chamber and pressed through a die to create a shape. Attention must be paid to the consistency of the dough, which will not extrude properly if it is too soft or too firm. This is the key to success with electric pasta machines.

Each electric pasta machine is different. One model may direct you to process the dough until barely moist pea-sized clumps are formed. Another model will insist that the dough will only work if it is evenly moistened and in walnut-sized pieces. *The dough must be processed according to the manufacturer's instruction booklet, as each brand's motor and dies require a different consistency.* Try as I might, I couldn't come up with a generic electric pasta machine pasta dough recipe that worked well in all models.

But I don't think this is a bad thing: No one expects a Ford carburetor to work in a Chevy.

The recipes in this chapter were developed for a Simac MX700. I chose this machine because Simac is a well-respected and well-represented name in kitchen appliances and its pasta machine has been on the market for a long time. (This should not be taken as an endorsement; all the machines have their own selling points.) You can easily adapt the recipes in this chapter according to the general instructions for your pasta machine to make the pasta dough as illustrated in its booklet. Here is a breakdown of the various machines with a sample recipe, so that you can see how different the machines are.

Simac MX700

Capacity: about 1½ pounds pasta. The basic egg pasta recipe uses 16 ounces (2 Simac cups) unbleached all-purpose flour and 4½ large eggs (or about 1 cup plus 2 tablespoons liquid egg substitute).

Dies: capellini, spaghetti, linguine, fettuccine, lasagne, macaroni, bucati, and cookies. You can special-order dies for many other shapes.

Desired dough consistency: Evenly moist, walnut-sized lumps.

Cuisinart DPM-3

Capacity: 3 pounds. Recipes are for 1½ pounds, but most can be doubled. They include a recipe for egg substitute pasta: 4 cups (20 ounces) unbleached all-purpose flour, 2 tablespoons oil, 1 teaspoon salt, and 1 cup egg substitute. The recipes can be used in this machine by increasing the flour to 4 cups total per batch.

Dies: capellini, spaghetti, penne, fettuccine, lasagne, gnocchi, and breadsticks.

Desired dough consistency: Evenly moist walnut-sized lumps.

Pasta Perfetto 900 (Vitantonio)

Capacity: 1½ pounds pasta. The basic egg pasta recipe calls for 16 ounces (2 Pasta Perfetto cups) all-purpose flour, ½ teaspoon salt (optional), 3½ large eggs (1¾ cups liquid egg substitute). The instructions say to add hot or warm water as necessary to reach the liquid level on the measuring cups; it is not necessary if large eggs are used.

Dies: Spaghetti, thick spaghetti, thin spaghetti, macaroni, fettuccine, lasagne, medium egg noodle, and rigatoni.

Desired dough consistency: Small pea-sized pieces of dough that, when pressed into a ball, will hold together without crumbling.

Pasta Express X2000 and X3000
(Creative Technologies Corporation)

Capacity: about 1½ pounds pasta. The basic all-eggs pasta recipe uses 16 ounces (2 Pasta Express cups) unbleached all-purpose flour, 2 teaspoons oil, 1 teaspoon salt (optional), and 4 large eggs (1 cup liquid egg substitute).

Dies: Spaghetti, linguine, ziti, lasagne, vermicelli, fettuccine, small macaroni, gnocchi, bagel, cookie, and pretzel/bread sticks. The X3000 comes with a large macaroni die, which can be special-ordered for the X2000.

Desired dough consistency: Pea-sized crumbles; dough is ready when pressed between the fingers, the whiteness of the flour disappears.

Popeil's Automatic Pasta Maker
(Popeil Pasta Products, Inc.)

Capacity: about 1½ pounds pasta. The machine works best with an egg-oil-water mixture: 16 ounces (2 Popeil cups) all-purpose flour, 2 large eggs (or ½ cup liquid egg substitute), 2 tablespoons olive oil, 1 teaspoon salt, and enough water to reach the marked level on their liquid measuring cup (about 6 tablespoons).

Dies: gnocchi, macaroni, tagliatelle, vermicelli, rigatoni, lasagne, linguine, angel hair, spaghetti, fettuccine, small bagel, and cookie. Also available by special order are penne, Oriental noodle, bagel and meatball, rugala, small cookie, manicotti, pappardelle, rotini, shell, pastry dough, bread stick, and fusilli.

Desired dough consistency: Small pea-sized lumps.

TIPS FOR MAKING PASTA IN AN
ELECTRIC PASTA MACHINE

- When you are first learning to use the electric pasta machine, make the easier doughs, such as Traditional Semolina and Egg Pasta (page 73).

Colored pastas are a little tricky—the thickness of the vegetable juice can make getting the right consistency a challenge. Once you are familiar with how the dough should look and feel under optimum conditions, try the more difficult doughs. (Not all the handmade pasta doughs in Chapter 3 have equivalents for the electric pasta machine; some are too difficult for the machine and not worth the effort.)

- Each machine uses its own measuring cups. These are *not* equivalent to the standard American household measuring cups. Most manufacturers suggest using their measures (dry *and* liquid) or using scales for dry ingredients. This is because most machines were developed in Europe, where the metric system of measuring is used. Only Cuisinart uses American measuring methods in its booklet. I use American measures in my recipes.
- Proportions of flour and liquid are always approximate, because of the varying moisture content of different flours, caused by the amount of humidity in the air or the exact grind or type of flour. You may find that you need to add a little more flour or water to reach the proper consistency.
- The electric pasta machines generally yield about one pound, five ounces of dough. Most of the recipes in this book call for one pound of pasta. Simply place the extra five ounces of pasta in a plastic bag and refrigerate for up to two days, or freeze for up to one month. This amount is perfect for two people.
- To help the dough extrude easily, soak the dies in warm water for at least one minute before attaching them to the machine. I also spray the die opening lightly with nonstick vegetable cooking spray to reduce the chance of sticking.
- Before adding the dry ingredients—including dry seasonings—to the mixing container, be sure the shutter slide is closed (if the machine has one) and that the machine is set on "mix," not on "extrude."
- After the pasta has mixed for about three minutes, turn off the machine. Use a wooden spoon to lift up and mix the dough that is at the bottom of the container. This step is particularly helpful with the Simac and Cuisinart machines. If the dough is too heavy and wet, use your hands to break the clumps into smaller pieces before sprinkling the dough with about a tablespoon of flour and mixing it again for about one minute. This helps distribute the flour evenly.
- The first twelve inches or so of extruded pasta may have rough edges. If so, either the dough is too dry or the dies are not properly lubricated. Normally, the rough edges smooth out as the machine extrudes more pasta, and the roughness is less noticeable when the pasta is cooked. If you are making tubular pasta, however, and the tubes are cracking, stop

the machine and adjust the dough consistency according to the manufacturer's instructions.

- Vegetable and fruit juices work better in extruder machines than the purees recommended by some manufacturers. It is difficult to mix a puree evenly with the other ingredients. If a recipe calls for a puree, such as a pesto, let it mix for at least three minutes before adding additional liquid. If you add the liquid too soon, you may end up with an overly wet dough. Use a juice extractor or puree the vegetables in a blender. To blend, place about two cups of the chopped vegetables in an electric blender with just enough water to lubricate them (anywhere from one half to one cup). Process on high for at least one minute, until liquified. Strain the mixture through a cheesecloth-lined wire sieve, pressing hard on the solids. Be aware that colored pastas rarely taste strongly of the vegetable used to tint the dough—the juices are used as dyes, not flavorings. (See page 28 for suggestions on how to increase the flavor in some pastas.) Use more of the same vegetable in the pasta sauce to emphasize it.

- Most of the electric pasta machine recipes include a small amount of oil, which improves the texture of the dough and helps intensify the flavor of any seasonings. The amount of oil is usually less than half a teaspoon per serving. You may choose to leave the oil out.

- Spiced pastas often include ingredients such as herbs, spices, or seeds, which may clog the dies. To avoid problems, first grind these ingredients in a mini-chopper or coffee grinder until very fine. To clean a coffee grinder to use as a spice grinder, grind half a cup of granulated sugar for one minute and then discard the sugar (or use it in coffee). The sugar will pick up any coffee flavor. Follow the same procedure to rid your machine of spicy flavors before you grind your next batch of coffee beans. Additionally, when making spiced pastas, choose dies with wide openings to reduce the chances of clogging.

- There is always a small piece of dough that collects in the workbowl and doesn't get extruded. Press the dough into the extrusion opening, and it will eventually extrude.

- See Drying the Dough (page 32) for complete instructions on how to handle the pasta after it comes out of the machine, plus storage tips. The information in How to Cook and Serve Pasta (page 14) refers to both handmade and extruded pastas.

- If you are considering buying an electric pasta machine, choose the one that has the fewest parts, since cleanup can be time-consuming. Cleaning will go more quickly if the different pieces are first allowed to air-dry overnight. (I cannot emphasize the importance of this hint enough: Let time do the work for you.) Any pasta dough on the pieces will harden but then can easily be flaked off or removed with the tip of a bamboo skewer. A bamboo skewer or push-pin is also necessary to poke the dough from the die holes. Do not soak parts that have pasta dough on them—it will only turn into a sticky mess. Be sure of your machine's dishwasher-safe status; obviously, the motor housing unit should never be immersed in water.

- Some pasta machine manufacturers include recipes for cookies, bread sticks, pastry dough, pretzels, corn chips, and other foods to make in their machines. Since this is a pasta book, I do not provide any recipes for these items. Follow the manufacturer's instructions if you want to try them; frankly, there wasn't one nonpasta recipe I tested in an extruder machine that I couldn't have made with less fuss and cleanup using only a bowl and a spoon. But, some disabled cooks may find it easier to make these items in an electric pasta machine, as they eliminate the need for rolling pins and other tools.

TRADITIONAL SEMOLINA AND EGG PASTA

Electric Machine Method

MAKES ABOUT 1 POUND, 4 OUNCES DOUGH

This golden-hued pasta is not only one of the most popular varieties, it is also easily made in the electric pasta machine. The machine likes the extra body provided by the strong semolina flour. This dough is particularly suited to tubular pastas, such as macaroni or penne. I give detailed steps in this recipe so that it can be used as a general guide for the other electric pasta machine recipes. Remember that this recipe was developed for a Simac MX 700, and different machines require different measurements of ingredients.

2 cups unbleached all-purpose flour
2 cups durum semolina (also called pasta flour)
¾ cup plus 2 tablespoons liquid egg substitute

1.   In the workbowl of an electric pasta machine, place the all-purpose and semolina flours (or any dry ingredients in other recipes), close the lid, and turn on the machine. With the machine running, over a 3-minute period, slowly pour in the liquid egg substitute (or combined liquids in other recipes) through the liquid feed opening. Continue to mix for 1 additional minute, then open the lid. Feel the dough to check for proper consistency (see pages 68 to 69). To adjust the consistency, add either more flour or more water, 1 tablespoon at a time, and mix for 1 minute after each addition, until the dough reaches the proper texture. Total mixing/kneading time should be about 7 minutes. (The total mixing/kneading time will vary from recipe to recipe and from machine to machine.)

2.   Meanwhile, soak the die you have selected in warm water for 2 minutes. Drain and spray lightly with vegetable nonstick cooking spray.

3.   Without the die in place, change the machine setting to "extrude," and let run for at least 45 seconds to extrude the first portion of pasta

dough, collecting this dough on a small plate. This first portion of extruded dough has a tendency to be dry, so don't panic. After about 45 seconds, the extruded dough should become moister and more supple. Turn off the machine and return the collected pasta dough to the workbowl.

4. Attach the die, turn on the machine, and begin to extrude the pasta shapes. With a sharp knife, cut the pasta into desired lengths as it extrudes, arranging the pasta in a single layer on a lightly floured baking sheet. The pasta may be used immediately. Or allow it to dry completely (1 to 2 hours, depending on the moistness of the dough and the weather), place in plastic bags, and refrigerate for up to 3 days.

Variation

SAFFRON PASTA

Mix 2 teaspoons crushed saffron threads into the liquid egg substitute.

NUTRITIONAL ANALYSIS PER SERVING (BASED ON 10 2-OUNCE SERVINGS)

CALORIES: 230 (17 percent from protein, 78 percent from carbohydrate, 5 percent from fat) • PROTEIN: 9 grams • CARBOHYDRATE: 44 grams • FAT: 1 gram • CHOLESTEROL: less than 1 milligram • SODIUM: 40 milligrams

CLASSIC EGG PASTA

Electric Machine Method

MAKES ABOUT 1 POUND, 4 OUNCES DOUGH

———

This is a tender, all-purpose pasta. Watch the consistency of the dough carefully to avoid adding too much liquid.

———

4 cups unbleached all-purpose flour
¾ cup plus 2 tablespoons liquid egg substitute

———

To make the pasta, follow the instructions on pages 73 to 74. Total mixing/kneading time should be about 7 minutes.

Variation

CURRY PASTA

Mix 3 tablespoons curry powder with 2 teaspoons vegetable oil. Add this paste to the flour in the workbowl before processing.

NUTRITIONAL ANALYSIS PER SERVING (BASED ON 10 2-OUNCE SERVINGS)
CALORIES: 200 (16 percent from protein, 78 percent from carbohydrate, 6 percent from fat) • PROTEIN: 8 grams • CARBOHYDRATE: 38 grams • FAT: 1 gram • CHOLESTEROL: less than 1 milligram • SODIUM: 40 milligrams

CHINESE WATER NOODLE DOUGH

Electric Machine Method

MAKES ABOUT 1 POUND, 5 OUNCES DOUGH

The dough to use for Asian recipes. You can vary the flavor by substituting one tablespoon dark Asian sesame oil for one tablespoon of the canola oil.

---

4 cups unbleached all-purpose flour
2 tablespoons canola or vegetable oil
¾ cup plus 2 tablespoons water

To make the pasta, follow the instructions on pages 73 to 74. Total mixing/kneading time should be about 7 minutes.

NUTRITIONAL ANALYSIS PER SERVING (BASED ON 8 SERVINGS)

CALORIES: 206 (10 percent from protein, 75 percent from carbohydrate, 15 percent from fat) •
PROTEIN: 5 grams • CARBOHYDRATE: 38 grams • FAT: 3 grams • CHOLESTEROL: 0 milligrams •
SODIUM: 1 milligram

WHOLE WHEAT PASTA

Electric Machine Method

MAKES ABOUT 1 POUND, 5 OUNCES DOUGH

Doughs with a high proportion of whole-grain flours are higher in gluten than other doughs and take a little longer to reach the proper consistency.

----

3 cups whole wheat flour
1 cup unbleached all-purpose flour
½ cup liquid egg substitute
6 tablespoons water, or more if needed

In the bowl of the electric pasta machine, combine the flours. In a liquid measuring cup, combine the liquid egg substitute and water. To make the pasta, follow the instructions on pages 73 to 74. Total mixing/kneading time should be about 8 minutes.

Variation

TRITICALE PASTA

Substitute 3 cups triticale flour for the whole wheat flour.

Variation

KAMUT PASTA

Substitute 3 cups kamut flour for the whole wheat flour.

(continued)

Variation

SPELT PASTA

Substitute 4 cups spelt flour for the all-purpose and whole wheat flours.

NUTRITIONAL ANALYSIS PER SERVING (BASED ON 10 2-OUNCE SERVINGS)
CALORIES: 178 (17 percent from protein, 77 percent from carbohydrate, 6 percent from fat) • PROTEIN: 8 grams • CARBOHYDRATE: 36 grams • FAT: 1 gram • CHOLESTEROL: less than 1 milligram • SODIUM: 24 milligrams

PUMPERNICKEL PASTA

Electric Machine Method

MAKES ABOUT 1 POUND, 6 OUNCES DOUGH

This is a delicious variation on the whole-grain pasta theme. Be sure to give it the slightly longer kneading time necessary for best results.

---

2 cups unbleached all-purpose flour
1 cup whole wheat flour
1 cup rye flour
1 tablespoon cocoa powder
2 teaspoons onion powder
¾ cup plus 2 tablespoons liquid egg substitute

In the bowl of the electric pasta machine, combine the flours, cocoa, and onion powder. To make the pasta, follow the instructions on pages 73 to 74. Total mixing/kneading time should be about 8 minutes.

> NUTRITIONAL ANALYSIS PER SERVING (BASED ON 11 2-OUNCE SERVINGS)
> CALORIES: 173 (17 percent from protein, 76 percent from carbohydrate, 7 percent from fat) • PROTEIN: 7 grams • CARBOHYDRATE: 33 grams • FAT: 1 gram • CHOLESTEROL: less than 1 milligram • SODIUM: 37 milligrams

GOLDEN CARROT PASTA

Electric Machine Method

MAKES ABOUT 1 POUND, 5 OUNCES DOUGH

Use vegetable juices as soon as possible after juicing, as their color dulls upon standing. Juices are used primarily for coloring, and you may find that the pasta does not have a particularly strong vegetable flavor. If you want to experiment with vegetable juices in egg-based pastas, be aware that the yellow color of the liquid egg substitute or the yolks will affect the final color of the pasta, sometimes adversely (beet pasta, for example, will turn out orange, not purple) and sometimes positively (heightening the orange in carrot pasta, for example).

---

²⁄₃ cup fresh carrot juice (from about 4 large carrots)
1 tablespoon canola oil
3¾ cups unbleached all-purpose flour

In a liquid measuring cup, mix the carrot juice and oil. To make the pasta, follow the instructions on pages 73 to 74. Total mixing/kneading time should be about 7 minutes.

Variation

CARROT GINGER PASTA

Add a 3-ounce piece of fresh ginger to the juicer or blender when juicing the carrots.

Variation

BRIGHT BEET PASTA

Substitute ⅔ cup fresh beet juice (from 12 ounces beets) for the carrot juice.

Variation

EMERALD GREEN PASTA

Substitute ⅔ cup spinach juice (from 1 pound fresh spinach) for the carrot juice.

Variation

MINTED ZUCCHINI PASTA

Substitute ⅔ cup fresh zucchini juice (from 2 large zucchini) for the carrot juice, and stir in 1 tablespoon crushed dried mint.

NUTRITIONAL ANALYSIS PER SERVING (BASED ON 10 2-OUNCE SERVINGS)

CALORIES: 195 (11 percent from protein, 80 percent from carbohydrate, 9 percent from fat) • PROTEIN: 5 grams • CARBOHYDRATE: 39 grams • FAT: 2 grams • CHOLESTEROL: 0 milligrams • SODIUM: 11 milligrams

SCALLION PANCAKE PASTA

Electric Machine Method

MAKES ABOUT I POUND, 4 OUNCES DOUGH

———

The herb mixture in this recipe provides color and flavor. For a subtle, spicy note, substitute one tablespoon hot sesame oil for one tablespoon of the plain sesame oil.

———

¾ cup chopped scallions, green part only (3 to 4 scallions)
¾ cup chopped fresh cilantro, leaves and stems
½ cup water
2 tablespoons dark Asian sesame oil
3¾ cups unbleached all-purpose flour

———

1. In a blender, puree the herbs with the water and oil until completely liquified, 1 minute or longer. Strain the mixture through a cheesecloth-lined sieve, pressing hard on the solids to extract as much liquid as possible. Measure the herb liquid, and add water if necessary to make ⅔ cup.

2. To make the pasta, follow the instructions on pages 73 to 74. Total mixing/kneading time should be about 7 minutes.

NUTRITIONAL ANALYSIS PER SERVING (BASED ON 10 2-OUNCE SERVINGS)

CALORIES: 189 (11 percent from protein, 79 percent from carbohydrate, 9 percent from fat) • PROTEIN: 5 grams • CARBOHYDRATE: 37 grams • FAT: 2 grams • CHOLESTEROL: 0 milligrams • SODIUM: 26 milligrams

FRESH GARDEN HERB PASTA

Electric Machine Method

MAKES ABOUT 1 POUND, 5 OUNCES DOUGH

———

A full-flavored pasta; you can use less garlic if you wish. For a pesto-like flavor, increase the basil to one and a half cups, and omit the parsley and chives. The basil "juice" in this recipe works more successfully in a machine than homemade pesto would.

———

¾ cup lightly packed fresh basil leaves, chopped
½ cup chopped fresh parsley
¼ cup chopped fresh chives
2 garlic cloves, crushed
⅔ cup water
1 tablespoon canola oil
2 cups durum semolina (also called pasta flour)
1¾ cups unbleached all-purpose flour

———

1. In a blender, puree the basil, parsley, chives, and garlic with the water and oil until completely liquified, at least 1 minute. Strain the mixture through a cheesecloth-lined sieve, pressing hard on the solids to extract as much liquid as possible. Measure the herb liquid, and add water if necessary to make ⅔ cup.

2. To make the pasta, follow the instructions on pages 73 to 74. Total mixing/kneading time should be 8 to 9 minutes.

NUTRITIONAL ANALYSIS PER SERVING (BASED ON 10 2-OUNCE SERVINGS)

CALORIES: 215 (13 percent from protein, 79 percent from carbohydrate, 9 percent from fat) •
PROTEIN: 7 grams • CARBOHYDRATE: 42 grams • FAT: 2 grams • CHOLESTEROL: 0 milligrams •
SODIUM: 3 milligrams

MARYLAND SPICE BOX PASTA

Electric Machine Method

MAKES ABOUT I POUND, 5 OUNCES DOUGH

———

Serve with just about any seafood pasta.

———

3¾ cups unbleached all-purpose flour
¼ cup Old Bay Seasoning
¾ cup water
2 teaspoons canola oil

———

In the workbowl of an electric pasta machine, combine the flour and seasoning mix. In a liquid measuring cup, combine the water and oil. To make the pasta, follow the instructions on pages 73 to 74. Total mixing/kneading time should be about 6 minutes.

NUTRITIONAL ANALYSIS PER SERVING (BASED ON 10 2-OUNCE SERVINGS)
CALORIES: 194 (16 percent from protein, 77 percent from carbohydrate, 7 percent from fat) • PROTEIN: 8 grams • CARBOHYDRATE: 37 grams • FAT: 1 gram • CHOLESTEROL: less than 1 milligram • SODIUM: 40 milligrams

GINGER CITRUS PASTA

Electric Machine Method

MAKES ABOUT 1 POUND, 5 OUNCES DOUGH

If desired, use three quarters of a cup water and a half teaspoon each of lemon and orange oils (see page 19). to replace the citrus zest and juice.

Zest and juice of 1 large orange, plus additional juice if necessary
Zest and juice of 2 large lemons
3 tablespoons ground ginger
1 tablespoon canola oil
3¾ cups unbleached all-purpose flour

---

1. Combine the orange and lemon juices in a liquid measuring cup. You should have ¾ cup; if necessary, add more orange juice. Set aside.

2. Combine the orange and lemon zest with the ginger and oil to make a paste. In the workbowl of an electric pasta machine, combine the flour and the zest mixture.

3. To make the pasta, follow the instructions on pages 73 to 74. Total mixing/kneading time should be about 6 minutes.

NUTRITIONAL ANALYSIS PER SERVING (BASED ON 10 2-OUNCE SERVINGS)
CALORIES: 195 (10 percent from protein, 80 percent from carbohydrate, 10 percent from fat) •
PROTEIN: 5 grams • CARBOHYDRATE: 39 grams • FAT: 2 grams • CHOLESTEROL: 0 milligrams •
SODIUM: 2 milligrams

Pasta Classics for Today's Healthful Kitchen

In the old days, fat equaled flavor. For example, I have recipes for a simple tomato and garlic sauce for a pound of pasta that has half a cup of olive oil; for a ragù for the same amount made with two pounds of ground pork; and for fettuccine Alfredo with two cups heavy cream, a stick of butter, four egg yolks, and two cups of grated Parmesan cheese.

Now, with new low-fat ingredients and a fresh approach, I have transformed these recipes into mouth-watering dishes that can fit into today's healthy life-style. These are still "Grandma" recipes, with old-fashioned taste—it's just that Grandma has gotten hip and lean!

Many of these dishes are so quick to prepare they could fit in the Dinner in the Time It Takes for the Water to Boil chapter: for example, Faux Fettuccine Alfredo, Coal Miner's Light Fettuccine, Thai Chicken-Basil Sauce with Linguine, Hot as Hades Pasta, and Spaghetti with Tomato-Vodka Sauce. Others are special-occasion or holiday dishes, like the Apricot-Raisin Kugel and the Kasha-Vegetable Varnishkes.

What I really love are those long-simmered sauces that fill the house with spicy aromas that tell your guests as soon as they walk in that something special is going to be served: Herbed Marinara Sauce with Linguine, Better-for-You Fettuccine Bolognese, Old-Fashioned Tomato "Gravy" on Penne, Turkey Ragù on Fettuccine, and Wild Mushroom Ragout Pasta. Any of these sauces can be prepared in advance, and refrigerated or frozen for impromptu meals.

LEAN PESTO LINGUINE

MAKES ABOUT 1 CUP PESTO; 6 TO 8 SERVINGS

Pesto is normally loaded with olive oil. While olive oil may have health benefits, it still has fat grams that must be tallied in your daily total. By substituting broth for the oil, you'll get a fantastic pesto packed with fresh basil flavor.

LEAN PESTO

2 cups packed fresh basil leaves
⅓ cup freshly grated imported Parmesan cheese
1 garlic clove, or more to taste
¼ teaspoon salt
¼ teaspoon freshly ground black pepper
⅓ cup chicken stock, preferably homemade (page 212), or low-sodium canned broth
1 pound freshly made or store-bought fresh cholesterol-free linguine

---

1. Make the pesto: In a food processor fitted with the metal blade, combine the basil, Parmesan cheese, garlic, salt, and pepper, and pulse until chopped. With the machine running, gradually add the chicken stock through the tube, scraping down the sides of the machine as needed, and process until smooth. (The pesto can be prepared up to 2 days ahead. Press a piece of plastic wrap directly on the surface of the pesto to discourage discoloration, and refrigerate.)

2. In a large pot of boiling salted water, cook the pasta until just tender, 2 to 3 minutes. Scoop ⅓ cup of the pasta cooking water out of the pot and set aside. Drain the pasta and return to the pot.

3. Add the pesto and the reserved cooking water, toss well, and serve.

NUTRITIONAL ANALYSIS PER SERVING (BASED ON 8 SERVINGS)

CALORIES: 247 (16 percent from protein, 76 percent from carbohydrate, 9 percent from fat) • PROTEIN: 9 grams • CARBOHYDRATE: 46 grams • FAT: 2 grams • CHOLESTEROL: 3 milligrams • SODIUM: 171 milligrams

---

FAUX FETTUCCINE ALFREDO

MAKES 6 TO 8 SERVINGS

Rich, creamy, unctuous fettuccine Alfredo is a culinary hedonist's dream. My rendition is all of these, but, surprisingly, devoid of heavy cream. Note that while liquid egg substitute is salmonella-free, egg whites are not, so don't be tempted to use whites as an alternative. The cooking time isn't long enough to kill any bacteria in the whites.

1⅓ cups (about 11 ounces) nonfat ricotta or cottage cheese
⅔ cup skim milk
½ cup freshly grated imported Parmesan cheese
¼ cup liquid egg substitute
⅛ teaspoon salt
⅛ teaspoon freshly ground black pepper
1 pound freshly made or store-bought fresh cholesterol-free
   fettuccine

---

1. In a blender or a food processor fitted with the metal blade, process the cottage cheese, skim milk, Parmesan cheese, liquid egg substitute, salt, and pepper until smooth. Set aside.

2. In a large pot of boiling salted water, cook the pasta until barely tender, 1 to 2 minutes. Drain well, and return to the pot.

3. Add the cheese sauce and toss well. Cook over low heat, stirring constantly, just until the cheese sauce is heated through, about 1 minute. Do not boil. Transfer to a warmed serving bowl and serve immediately.

NUTRITIONAL ANALYSIS PER SERVING (BASED ON 8 SERVINGS)

CALORIES: 240 (26 percent from protein, 58 percent from carbohydrate, 16 percent from fat) • PROTEIN: 15 grams • CARBOHYDRATE: 34 grams • FAT: 4 grams • CHOLESTEROL: 7 milligrams • SODIUM: 191 milligrams

---

HERBED MARINARA SAUCE
WITH LINGUINE

MAKES ABOUT 5 CUPS SAUCE; 6 TO 8 SERVINGS

Perhaps the ultimate pasta classic is ribbons of fresh noodles dressed with a tangy, herb-flecked, long-simmered tomato sauce. This chunky marinara sauce is a kitchen standard that you will use again and again. (If you want a smooth sauce, pulse the finished marinara in a food processor to your desired consistency.) Using both fresh and canned tomatoes is a trick divulged by an excellent Italian cook. But if the plum tomatoes available aren't perfect, use canned tomatoes in juice along with those in puree. I urge you to make the sauce in large quantities and freeze it in one pint containers for future meals.

HERBED MARINARA SAUCE

2 teaspoons olive oil
1 medium onion, finely chopped
1 garlic clove, minced
2 pounds ripe medium plum tomatoes, seeded and chopped, or 1
    28-ounce can tomatoes in juice, undrained
1 28-ounce can tomatoes in thick puree, undrained
2 tablespoons chopped fresh basil or 2 tablespoons dried basil
1 tablespoon chopped fresh oregano or 1½ teaspoons dried oregano
2 teaspoons chopped fresh rosemary or 1 teaspoon dried rosemary
¼ teaspoon freshly ground black pepper

1 pound freshly made or store-bought fresh cholesterol-free linguine
6 tablespoons to ½ cup freshly grated imported Parmesan cheese

---

· MR. PASTA'S HEALTHY PASTA COOKBOOK ·

1. Make the marinara sauce: In a large saucepan, heat the oil over medium-low heat. Add the onion and garlic and cook, stirring often, until the onion is golden, about 5 minutes. Stir in the tomatoes, with their juices and puree, the herbs, if using dried, and the pepper. (Do not add the fresh herbs at this point, as their flavor would diminish during long cooking.) Bring to a simmer over medium-high heat, breaking up the tomatoes with the side of a spoon. Reduce the heat to low and cook, stirring often, until the sauce has thickened and reduced to about 5 cups, about 1½ hours. If using fresh herbs, stir in during the last 10 minutes of cooking. (The sauce can be prepared ahead, cooled, covered, and refrigerated up to 3 days or frozen up to 2 months. Reheat, thawed, if necessary, over low heat before serving.)

2. Meanwhile, in a large pot of boiling salted water, cook the pasta until just tender, 2 to 3 minutes. Drain and return to the pot.

3. Add the marinara sauce and mix well. Transfer to a warmed serving bowl and serve immediately, sprinkling each serving with 1 tablespoon Parmesan cheese.

NUTRITIONAL ANALYSIS PER SERVING (BASED ON 8 SERVINGS)

CALORIES: 269 (16 percent from protein, 65 percent from carbohydrate, 19 percent from fat) • PROTEIN: 11 grams • CARBOHYDRATE: 45 grams • FAT: 6 grams • CHOLESTEROL: 5 milligrams • SODIUM: 306 milligrams

COAL MINER'S LIGHT FETTUCCINE

MAKES 6 TO 8 SERVINGS

F ettuccine carbonara is a healthy eater's nightmare—bacon, heavy cream, and egg yolks. (It is named for northern Italy's coal miners, who need plenty of sustenance.) When I made this updated version for my friends, they pronounced it one of the best they'd ever had—with no idea that what they were enjoying had only a fraction of the fat found in the classic carbonara.

4 ounces Canadian bacon, cut into strips 1 inch long
and ¼ inch thick
1½ cups (12 ounces) nonfat cottage or ricotta cheese
¾ cup evaporated skimmed milk
½ cup liquid egg substitute
¼ teaspoon salt
1 pound freshly made or store-bought fresh cholesterol-free
fettuccine
¼ teaspoon freshly ground black pepper, or more to taste
6 tablespoons to ½ cup freshly grated imported Parmesan cheese

1. In a medium nonstick skillet, cook the Canadian bacon over medium heat, stirring occasionally, until lightly browned. Transfer to a plate and set aside.

2. In a blender, process the cottage cheese, evaporated milk, egg substitute, and salt until smooth. Set aside.

3. In a large pot of boiling salted water, cook the pasta until barely tender, 1 to 2 minutes. Drain well and return to the pot.

4. Add the cheese mixture, bacon, and pepper to the pasta and cook over medium-low heat, stirring constantly, just until the sauce is heated through, about 1 minute. Do not boil. Transfer to a warmed serving bowl. Serve immediately, sprinkling each serving with 1 tablespoon Parmesan cheese.

NUTRITIONAL ANALYSIS PER SERVING (BASED ON 8 SERVINGS)

CALORIES: 286 (30 percent from protein, 52 percent from carbohydrate, 18 percent from fat) • PROTEIN: 21 grams • CARBOHYDRATE: 36 grams • FAT: 6 grams • CHOLESTEROL: 16 milligrams • SODIUM: 472 milligrams

BETTER-FOR-YOU FETTUCCINE BOLOGNESE

MAKES ABOUT 5 CUPS SAUCE; 6 TO 8 SERVINGS

There are as many versions of Bolognese sauce as there are Italian cooks. Pork, veal, beef, heavy cream, wine, and tomatoes all come into play in a variety of configurations. This version uses turkey sausage with a fillip of evaporated skimmed milk to produce a healthful, mouth-watering sauce.

BOLOGNESE SAUCE

Nonstick vegetable cooking spray
3 sweet Italian turkey sausages (about 7 ounces), casings removed
1 medium onion, finely chopped
1 medium carrot, finely chopped
1 medium celery rib, finely chopped
1 garlic clove, minced
2 28-ounce cans tomatoes in juice, drained and chopped
½ cup dry white wine
2 tablespoons tomato paste
1 teaspoon dried rosemary
1 teaspoon dried basil
¼ teaspoon freshly ground black pepper
¾ cup evaporated skimmed milk

1 pound freshly made or store-bought fresh cholesterol-free
  fettuccine

----

1. Spray a large nonstick skillet with nonstick vegetable spray, and heat over medium heat. Add the turkey sausage, onion, carrot, celery, and garlic and cook, stirring often to break up the sausage, until the meat has lost its pink color, about 5 minutes. Transfer to a medium saucepan.

2. Add the tomatoes, wine, tomato paste, rosemary, basil, and pepper, and bring to a boil over medium-high heat. Reduce the heat to low, and simmer until the sauce has thickened slightly and reduced to about 5

cups, about 1 hour and 15 minutes. Add the evaporated milk and simmer for 5 minutes. (The sauce can be prepared ahead, cooled, covered, and refrigerated for up to 3 days or frozen for up to 1 month. Reheat, defrosted if necessary, over low heat before using.)

3. Meanwhile, in a large pot of boiling salted water, cook the pasta until just tender, 2 to 3 minutes. Drain and return to the pot.

4. Add the sauce, toss well, and serve immediately.

NUTRITIONAL ANALYSIS PER SERVING (BASED ON 8 SERVINGS)

CALORIES: 300 (19 percent from protein, 64 percent from carbohydrate, 13 percent from fat) • PROTEIN: 15 grams • CARBOHYDRATE: 49 grams • FAT: 4 grams • CHOLESTEROL: 17 milligrams • SODIUM: 618 milligrams

OVEN-BAKED TURKEY-SPINACH MEATBALLS AND SPAGHETTI

MAKES 6 TO 8 SERVINGS

Using a combination of turkey sausage and spinach adds interest and good health to the standard fat-laden meatball. When choosing ground turkey, pick a variety with 7 percent fat or less. Cheap brands often have up to 15 percent fat, which is the same as beef ground round! I find it much easier to bake a large batch of meatballs rather than cook them on top of the stove—not only are they easier to turn for even browning, I can use less fat. Once they are baked, I toss the turkey meatballs with homemade sauce and serve with spaghetti for a hearty Old Country meal.

Nonstick vegetable cooking spray
½ cup fresh bread crumbs
¼ cup skim milk
¼ cup liquid egg substitute or 2 large egg whites
1 small onion, minced
1 garlic clove, minced
1 teaspoon dried basil
1 teaspoon dried rosemary
½ teaspoon salt
¼ teaspoon freshly ground black pepper
1 pound sweet Italian turkey sausage, casings removed, crumbled
1 10-ounce package frozen spinach, thawed and squeezed dry
1 pound dried spaghetti
1 recipe Herbed Marinara Sauce (page 90), heated

1. Preheat the oven to 350°F. Lightly spray a baking sheet with nonstick vegetable spray.

2. In a medium bowl, soak the bread crumbs in the skim milk for 5 minutes. Then stir in the egg substitute, onion, garlic, basil, rosemary, salt, and pepper. Add the ground turkey and spinach and mix well, with your hands.

3. Shape into 18 meatballs and place about 1 inch apart on the prepared baking sheet. Bake, carefully turning once, until the meatballs are cooked through and lightly browned, about 25 minutes.

4. Meanwhile, in a large pot of boiling salted water, cook the pasta until just tender, about 7 minutes. Drain and return to the pot.

5. Add half of the hot sauce to the spaghetti and toss well. Transfer to a large warmed serving bowl. Top with the meatballs, pour the remaining sauce over, and serve immediately.

NUTRITIONAL ANALYSIS PER SERVING (BASED ON 8 SERVINGS)
CALORIES: 377 (23 percent from protein, 55 percent from carbohydrate, 22 percent from fat) • PROTEIN: 22 grams • CARBOHYDRATE: 52 grams • FAT: 10 grams • CHOLESTEROL: 50 milligrams • SODIUM: 627 milligrams

OLD-FASHIONED TOMATO "GRAVY" ON PENNE

MAKES ABOUT 7 CUPS SAUCE; 8 TO 12 SERVINGS

———

Many Italian-American households sauce their pasta with a tomato "gravy," which differs from a tomato "sauce" in its use of meat and broth to add depth of flavor. Usually, pork neck bones are utilized (the butcher's case in my Italian neighborhood is piled high with them), but I find leaner chicken thighs work beautifully. This makes a large batch of sauce, for enough pasta to feed a crowd. If you want to sauce only a pound of pasta, use five cups of the sauce and freeze the remainder for another meal.

———

6 chicken thighs (about 2 pounds)
2 teaspoons olive oil
1 medium onion, chopped
2 garlic cloves, finely chopped
1 celery rib, finely chopped
1 carrot, finely chopped
4 ounces fresh mushrooms, sliced
1 28-ounce can tomato puree
1 6-ounce can tomato paste
2 cups chicken stock, preferably homemade (page 212), or
* low sodium canned broth*
¾ cup red wine
¼ cup chopped fresh parsley
1 tablespoon dried oregano
2 teaspoons dried basil
1 teaspoon dried rosemary
½ teaspoon dried thyme
1 bay leaf
¼ teaspoon crushed hot red pepper
1½ pounds dried penne or other tubular pasta

———

1. Heat a large dry saucepan over medium-high heat. Add the chicken thighs, skin side down, and cook until the skin is golden brown, about 4 minutes. Turn and brown the other side, about 3 minutes. Transfer to a plate and set aside. Pour off all of the fat and wipe out the saucepan with paper towels, but leave any browned bits in the bottom of the pan.

2. Set the saucepan over medium heat and add the oil. Add the onion, garlic, celery, carrot, and mushrooms. Cover and cook, stirring occasionally, until the vegetables are almost tender, about 5 minutes.

3. Stir in the tomato puree, tomato paste, chicken stock, wine, parsley, oregano, basil, rosemary, thyme, bay leaf, and crushed red pepper. Add the reserved chicken thighs, and bring to a simmer. Reduce the heat to low and cook, stirring occasionally, for 1½ hours, or until the sauce is evaporated to about 7 cups. Remove from the heat. Transfer the chicken thighs to a plate and cool slightly.

4. Remove the skin and bones from the chicken, coarsely chop the meat, and stir the chicken meat into the sauce. Skim off any fat on the surface of the sauce. Cool the sauce to room temperature, then cover and refrigerate for at least 4 hours. (The sauce can be prepared ahead and refrigerated up to 3 days or frozen up to 2 months.)

5. Lift off any hardened fat on the surface of the sauce, and reheat the sauce over low heat.

6. Meanwhile, in a large pot of boiling salted water, cook the pasta until just tender, about 8 minutes. Drain and return to the pot.

7. Add the sauce and toss well. Transfer to a warmed large serving bowl and serve immediately.

NUTRITIONAL ANALYSIS PER SERVING (BASED ON 12 SERVINGS)

CALORIES: 294 (25 percent from protein, 59 percent from carbohydrate, 13 percent from fat) • PROTEIN: 19 grams • CARBOHYDRATE: 44 grams • FAT: 4 grams • CHOLESTEROL: 47 milligrams • SODIUM: 549 milligrams

TURKEY RAGÙ ON FETTUCCINE

MAKES ABOUT 5 CUPS SAUCE; 6 TO 8 SERVINGS

The indication that a ragù must be a meaty sauce is in its name, which is from the French word *ragoût,* meaning "stew." Old-fashioned ragùs are made with ground beef, pork, and/or veal, but by using lean ground turkey breast (only 1 percent fat), you can create a hearty sauce while trimming the fat. If you can't find ground turkey breast (look carefully at the label, as this is different from regular ground turkey), you can purchase boneless, skinless turkey breast and grind it yourself in the food processor. Regular ground turkey will work, but the fat content is higher.

Nonstick vegetable cooking spray
1 pound lean ground turkey breast
1 medium onion, minced
1 carrot, minced
1 celery rib, minced
8 ounces fresh mushrooms, finely chopped
1 garlic clove, minced
1 28-ounce can tomatoes in juice, drained and chopped
1 cup chicken stock, preferably homemade (page 212), or
  low sodium canned broth
½ cup dry white wine
¼ cup chopped fresh parsley
2 tablespoons tomato paste
½ teaspoon dried sage
½ teaspoon dried rosemary
¼ teaspoon freshly ground black pepper
1 pound freshly made or store-bought fresh cholesterol-free
  fettuccine

------

1. Spray a large nonstick skillet lightly with nonstick vegetable spray. Add the turkey, onion, carrot, celery, mushrooms, and garlic and cook over medium heat, stirring often to break up the ground turkey, until the turkey loses its pink color, about 5 minutes. Transfer to a medium saucepan.

2. Stir in the tomatoes, stock, wine, parsley, tomato paste, sage, rosemary, and pepper. Bring to a simmer and cook over low heat, stirring occasionally, until slightly thickened, about 1 hour. (The sauce can be prepared ahead, cooled, covered, and refrigerated up to 3 days or frozen up to 2 months. Reheat, defrosted if necessary, over low heat before using.)

3. Meanwhile, in a large pot of boiling salted water, cook the pasta until just tender, 2 to 3 minutes. Drain and return to the pot.

4. Add the sauce and toss well. Transfer to a warmed serving bowl and serve immediately.

NUTRITIONAL ANALYSIS PER SERVING (BASED ON 8 SERVINGS)

CALORIES: 310 (33 percent from protein, 55 percent from carbohydrate, 9 percent from fat) • PROTEIN: 26 grams • CARBOHYRATE: 43 grams • FAT: 3 grams • CHOLESTEROL: 47 milligrams • SODIUM: 338 milligrams

HOT AS HADES PASTA

MAKES 6 TO 8 SERVINGS

———

This is a low-fat version of pasta all'amatriciana, which is usually made as hot as the cook can stand. Interestingly, Italians rarely cook with fresh hot peppers, although dried red peppers and pickled green peppers (*peperoncini*) are popular. Serve this with a very sturdy red wine, such as a Zinfandel.

———

1 teaspoon olive oil
4 ounces Canadian bacon coarsely chopped (about 1 cup)
2 garlic cloves, minced
1 28-ounce can crushed tomatoes in puree
2 tablespoons chopped pickled peppers (peperoncini*)*
1 teaspoon dried oregano
¼ teaspoon crushed hot red pepper, or more to taste
1 pound dried long macaroni, such as bucatini
6 tablespoons to ½ cup freshly grated imported Parmesan cheese

———

1. In a large nonstick skillet, heat the oil over medium heat. Add the bacon and garlic and cook, stirring often, until the bacon is lightly browned, about 3 minutes. Stir in the tomatoes, pickled peppers, oregano, and crushed hot pepper. Bring to a simmer, reduce the heat to low, and cook until slightly thickened, about 5 minutes.

2. Meanwhile, in a large pot of boiling salted water, cook the pasta until just tender, about 9 minutes. Drain and return to the pot.

3. Add the sauce to the pasta, toss well, and transfer to a warmed serving bowl. Serve immediately, sprinkling each serving with 1 tablespoon Parmesan cheese.

NUTRITIONAL ANALYSIS PER SERVING (BASED ON 8 SERVINGS)

CALORIES: 317 (19 percent from protein, 68 percent from carbohydrate, 14 percent from fat) • PROTEIN: 15 grams • CARBOHYDRATE: 53 grams • FAT: 5 grams • CHOLESTEROL: 13 milligrams • SODIUM: 613 milligrams

---

PENNE WITH SMOTHERED KALE AND NEW POTATOES

MAKES 6 TO 8 SERVINGS

The robust, bold flavor of greens such as kale is tempered with long cooking. In many recipes, pork fat acts as a seasoning, but lean Canadian bacon is a fine stand-in.

1 bunch curly dark kale (about 1 pound)
2 teaspoons olive oil
3 ounces Canadian bacon, cut into ¼-inch cubes
2 garlic cloves, minced
¼ teaspoon crushed hot red pepper
1 cup chicken stock, preferably homemade (page 212), or
    low-sodium canned broth
6 small new potatoes, (about 1 pound), well scrubbed
1 pound dried penne or other tubular pasta
1 tablespoon balsamic vinegar, or more to taste

(continued)

1. Cut the kale leaves crosswise into 2-inch strips, and coarsely chop the stems. Drop into a sink filled with cool water and agitate briskly with your hands. Lift the leaves and stems from the water and transfer to a bowl, leaving any dirt and grit in the bottom of the sink. Set aside.

2. In a Dutch oven, heat the oil over medium heat. Add the Canadian bacon and garlic and cook, stirring often, until the garlic is golden, about 2 minutes. Add the cleaned kale in batches, covering the pan and waiting for each batch to wilt before adding the next batch. Add the chicken stock and crushed red pepper, cover, and simmer until the kale is meltingly tender, about 1 hour.

3. Meanwhile, in a large saucepan of boiling salted water, cook the new potatoes until just tender when pierced with the tip of a sharp knife, 15 to 20 minutes. Drain, rinse under cool running water, and drain again. Cut into 1-inch pieces, and keep warm, covered loosely with aluminum foil.

4. In a large pot of boiling salted water, cook the penne until just tender, about 8 minutes. Drain well and return to the pot.

5. Add the hot kale and potatoes to the pasta and toss well. Sprinkle with the balsamic vinegar and toss again. Transfer to a warmed serving dish and serve immediately.

NUTRITIONAL ANALYSIS PER SERVING (BASED ON 8 SERVINGS)

CALORIES: 331 (15 percent from protein, 75 percent from carbohydrate, 10 percent from fat) • PROTEIN: 13 grams • CARBOYDRATE: 62 grams • FAT: 4 grams • CHOLESTEROL: 6 milligrams • SODIUM: 268 milligrams

ROASTED TOMATO SAUCE
OVER LINGUINE

MAKES 6 TO 8 SERVINGS

Roasting intensifies the naturally sweet/tangy flavor of ripe tomatoes. Make this at the end of tomato season, when the tomatoes are still plump and red, but the evenings are cool enough to turn on the oven.

1 tablespoon olive oil
2 garlic cloves, minced
4 pounds ripe medium plum tomatoes, halved lengthwise
1 pound freshly made or store-bought fresh cholesterol-free linguine
1 cup chopped fresh basil
½ teaspoon salt
¼ teaspoon freshly ground black pepper
6 tablespoons to ½ cup freshly grated imported Parmesan cheese

1. Preheat the oven to 500°F.

2. In a small bowl, mix the oil and garlic. Set aside.

3. Place the tomatoes on two baking sheets, cut sides up. Roast the tomatoes for 15 minutes, then switch the positions of the baking sheets from top to bottom and continue roasting until the cut surfaces of the tomatoes are lightly browned and the skins are slightly charred, about 30 minutes. During the last 5 minutes of cooking, brush with the garlic oil.

4. Meanwhile, in a large pot of boiling salted water, cook the pasta until just tender, 2 to 3 minutes. Drain and return to the pot.

5. Add the roasted tomatoes, basil, salt, and pepper to the pasta and toss well. Transfer to a warmed serving bowl and serve immediately, sprinkling each serving with 1 tablespoon Parmesan cheese.

NUTRITIONAL ANALYSIS PER SERVING (BASED ON 8 SERVINGS)

CALORIES: 288 (17 percent from protein, 65 percent from carbohydrate, 18 percent from fat) • PROTEIN: 12 grams • CARBOHYDRATE: 48 grams • FAT: 6 grams • CHOLESTEROL: 54 milligrams • SODIUM: 279 milligrams

CLAMS AND SPAGHETTI IN WHITE WINE SAUCE

MAKES 6 TO 8 SERVINGS

This clam sauce is vibrantly flavored with a good dash of oregano and red pepper. The smaller your clams are, the better—they shouldn't be more than two inches across. On the East Coast, this means littlenecks; on the West Coast, use Manila clams. I always soak my clams (and mussels) in a large bowl of salted water for thirty minutes to rid them of any sand. If the water in the bottom of the bowl is sandy after standing, repeat the procedure with fresh salted water until the water is clear.

---

2 garlic cloves, minced
1 tablespoon olive oil
½ cup bottled clam juice
½ cup dry white wine
2 tablespoons chopped fresh oregano or 2 teaspoons dried oregano
¼ teaspoon crushed hot red pepper, or more to taste
4 dozen small clams, well scrubbed, soaked, and drained
(see above)
1 pound dried spaghetti
½ cup chopped fresh parsley

---

1. In a large pot, cook the garlic in the oil over medium heat, stirring often, until the garlic is barely golden, about 2 minutes. Add the clam juice, white wine, oregano, and hot pepper, bring to a simmer. Reduce the heat to low and cook, partially covered, for 5 minutes. Add the clams, increase the heat to high, cover, and cook until the clams have opened, about 3 minutes. Discard any clams that do not open.

2. Meanwhile, in a large pot of boiling salted water, cook the pasta until just tender, about 7 minutes. Drain and return to the pot.

3. Add the clam sauce and parsley to the pasta and toss well. Cover the pot and let stand for 2 minutes to allow the pasta to absorb some of the sauce. Transfer to a warmed serving platter and serve immediately.

NUTRITIONAL ANALYSIS PER SERVING (BASED ON 8 SERVINGS)

CALORIES: 288 (19 percent from protein, 67 percent from carbohydrate, 10 percent from fat) • PROTEIN: 13 grams • CARBOHYDRATE: 48 grams • FAT: 3 grams • CHOLESTEROL: 14 milligrams • SODIUM: 107 milligrams

APRICOT-RAISIN KUGEL

MAKES 8 SERVINGS

————

Before I moved to New York from San Francisco, I had never tasted kugel, one of the mainstays of the Jewish-American holiday dinner table. This recipe employs secrets I culled from my assistant Jackie's grandmother, and I believe that even a traditionalist like herself would never know that my pudding has been made low-fat thanks to a few secrets of my own. You don't have to be Jewish to love kugel. Served with a fresh fruit salad and some sautéed turkey sausage, kugel is a welcome interdenominational brunch dish served at any time of the year.

————

Nonstick vegetable cooking spray
1 pound dried cholesterol-free noodles
1 cup (8 ounces) nonfat cottage cheese
1 8-ounce package "lite" cream cheese, at room temperature
½ cup skim milk
¾ cup liquid egg substitute or 6 large egg whites
½ cup granulated sugar
Grated zest of 1 lemon
½ teaspoon ground cinnamon (optional)
½ cup raisins or currants
½ cup sugarless apricot fruit spread (or your favorite flavor)

————

(continued)

1. Preheat the oven to 350°F. Lightly spray an 11- by 7-inch baking dish with nonstick cooking spray.

2. In a large pot of boiling salted water, cook the noodles until barely tender, about 7 minutes. (Do not overcook, as the noodles will cook further during baking.) Drain well, rinse under cold water, and drain again. Transfer to a large bowl.

3. In a blender or a food processor fitted with the metal blade, process the cottage cheese, cream cheese, skim milk, egg substitute, sugar, lemon zest, and optional cinnamon until smooth, scraping down the sides of the container with a spatula as needed. Pour the mixture over the drained noodles, add the raisins, and mix well. Transfer to the prepared baking dish. Drop dollops of the apricot spread over the top of the kugel.

4. Bake until the kugel is set and the top is golden brown and crusty, about 45 minutes. Let stand for 5 minutes before serving. Serve hot, warm, or at room temperature.

NUTRITIONAL ANALYSIS PER SERVING

CALORIES: 425 (17 percent from protein, 69 percent from carbohydrates, 14 percent from fat) • PROTEIN: 18 grams • CARBOHYDRATE: 75 grams • FAT: 7 grams • CHOLESTEROL: 17 milligrams • SODIUM: 229 milligrams

---

BROCCOLI RABE AND SAUSAGE WITH ZITI

MAKES 6 TO 8 SERVINGS

———

In my very Old World Italian neighborhood, the appearance of broccoli rabe (also known as broccoli di rapi or rape) is one of the first signs of autumn. Broccoli rabe is not unlike curly kale, but it has distinctive broccoli-like florets peeking out between the leaves. Turkey sausage, garlic, and hot red peppers stand up to broccoli rabe's sturdy flavor. (If you have a pasta pot with a perforated insert for draining, you can use the water that you use for the broccoli rabe to cook the pasta.)

———

2 pounds broccoli rabe, well rinsed
1 cup chicken stock, preferably homemade (see page 212), or
* low-sodium canned broth*
8 ounces sweet Italian turkey sausages, casings removed
3 garlic cloves, minced
¼ teaspoon salt
½ teaspoon crushed hot red pepper
1 pound dried ziti or other tubular pasta

———

1. Cut the broccoli rabe stems crosswise into ½-inch-wide pieces. Coarsely chop the florets and leaves.

2. In a large saucepan of boiling lightly salted water, cook the broccoli rabe over high heat until very tender, 15 to 20 minutes. Drain well.

3. In a large nonstick skillet, combine the chicken stock, turkey sausage, garlic, salt, and crushed red pepper and bring to a simmer over medium heat. Cook, breaking up the sausage with a wooden spoon, until the meat loses its pink color, about 5 minutes. Add the drained broccoli rabe, reduce the heat to low, and simmer, covered, for 5 minutes. (The sauce can be prepared up to 1 hour ahead. Reheat over low heat before serving.)

3. Meanwhile, in a large pot of boiling salted water, cook the pasta until just tender, about 8 minutes. Drain well and return to the pot.

4. Add the hot sauce, toss well, and serve immediately.

NUTRITIONAL ANALYSIS PER SERVING (BASED ON 8 SERVINGS)

CALORIES: 305 (21 percent from protein, 68 percent from carbohydrate, 11 percent from fat) • PROTEIN: 16 grams • CARBOHYDRATE: 53 grams • FAT: 4 grams • CHOLESTEROL: 18 milligrams • SODIUM: 424 milligrams

WILD MUSHROOM RAGOUT PASTA

MAKES 6 TO 8 SERVINGS

Most greengrocers now carry a whole medley of mushrooms. Few of these are truly "wild," but they do have a deeper woodsy flavor than ordinary white mushrooms. For best results, use at least two different varieties, and slice them lengthwise, unless you use shiitakes, so the shape and character of each type is recognizable. If you use shiitake mushrooms, discard the tough stems and slice the caps. If you make your own pasta for this dish, Wild Mushroom Pasta (page 48) is a great choice.

2 teaspoons olive oil
1 large onion, chopped
2 garlic cloves, minced
1½ pounds assorted fresh wild mushrooms, such as cremini,
    portobello, chanterelle, and oyster, trimmed and sliced
¾ cup chicken stock, preferably homemade (page 212), or
    low-sodium canned broth
¾ cup red wine
2 tablespoons Sun-dried Tomato Pesto (page 189) or tomato paste
3 tablespoons chopped fresh parsley
2 teaspoons chopped fresh sage or ¾ teaspoon crumbled dried sage
1 teaspoon chopped fresh rosemary or ½ teaspoon dried rosemary
1 teaspoon fresh marjoram or ½ teaspoon dried marjoram
½ teaspoon salt
¼ teaspoon freshly ground black pepper
1 pound freshly made or store-bought fresh cholesterol-free
    fettuccine
6 to 8 tablespoons freshly grated imported Parmesan cheese

1. In a large nonstick frying pan, heat the oil over medium-low heat. Add the onion and garlic and cook, stirring, until the onions are golden, about 5 minutes. Add the mushrooms, stock, wine, pesto, parsley, sage, rosemary, marjoram, salt, and pepper. Bring to a simmer, cover, and cook until the mushrooms are very tender, about 20 minutes.

2. Meanwhile, in a large pot of boiling salted water, cook the pasta until just tender, 2 to 3 minutes. Drain and return to the pot.

3. Add the sauce to the pasta and toss well. Transfer to a warmed serving bowl and serve immediately, sprinkling each serving with 1 tablespoon Parmesan cheese.

NUTRITIONAL ANALYSIS PER SERVING (BASED ON 8 SERVINGS)

CALORIES: 284 (15 percent from protein, 63 percent from carbohydrate, 17 percent from fat) • PROTEIN: 11 grams • CARBOHYDRATE: 46 grams • FAT: 5 grams • CHOLESTEROL: 5 milligrams • SODIUM: 355 milligrams

ESCAROLE AND WHITE BEANS WITH PENNE

MAKES 6 TO 8 SERVINGS

———

Besides the fact that this dish just plain tastes good, there are also health considerations for adding it to your menu. Not only are greens like escarole a great match with pasta, they are excellent sources of fiber, vitamins A and C, and folic acid (a B vitamin necessary for healthy red blood cells). And beans, also fiber-rich, are powerhouses of low-fat protein.

———

1 head garlic
1 medium onion, chopped
2 teaspoons olive oil
2 cups chicken stock, preferably homemade (page 212), or
 low-sodium canned broth
2 medium heads escarole (1½ pounds), well rinsed and cut into
 1-inch pieces
¼ teaspoon salt
¼ teaspoon crushed hot red pepper
1 cup cooked cannellini (white kidney) beans or 1 16-ounce can
 beans, drained and rinsed
1 pound dried penne or other tubular pasta

———

1. Preheat the oven to 400°F.

2. Loosely wrap the head of garlic in aluminum foil. Bake until the garlic is soft when squeezed (protect your hands with a kitchen towel), about 20 minutes, depending on the size of the head. Unwrap the garlic and allow to cool slightly.

3. Cut the garlic in half horizontally, and squeeze the softened pulp onto a small plate. Mash the garlic pulp with a fork into a puree.

4. In a large saucepan, heat the oil over medium-low heat. Add the onion and cook, covered, until softened, about 3 minutes. Add the stock, increase the heat to medium-high, and bring to a boil. Add the escarole in batches, covering and waiting for one batch to wilt before adding the next.

5. Add the garlic puree, salt, and crushed red pepper to the escarole. Reduce the heat to low, cover, and simmer until the escarole is tender, about 15 minutes. Add the beans and cook until heated through, about 5 minutes.

6. Meanwhile, in a large pot of boiling salted water, cook the pasta until just tender, about 8 minutes. Drain and return to the pot.

7. Add the escarole and beans to the pasta and toss well. Transfer to a warmed serving bowl and serve immediately.

NUTRITIONAL ANALYSIS PER SERVING (BASED ON 8 SERVINGS)

CALORIES: 300 (16 percent from protein, 75 percent from carbohydrate, 9 percent from fat) • PROTEIN: 12 grams • CARBOHYDRATE: 59 grams • FAT: 3 grams • CHOLESTEROL: 0 milligrams • SODIUM: 332 milligrams

KASHA-VEGETABLE VARNISHKES

MAKES 6 TO 8 SERVINGS

―――

Although kasha varnishkes is usually served as a side dish, I have transformed it into an entrée with a goodly amount of vegetables. Kasha is nothing more exotic than hulled, milled buckwheat groats (seeds). It comes in coarse, medium, and fine granulations—the coarse is best for this dish. Buckwheat is another fiber-filled, high-protein grain that most of us should become more familiar with—for reasons of both taste and health. Be sure to add boiling stock to the kasha mixture or it will become soggy.

―――

1 cup coarse kasha
¼ cup liquid egg substitute or 2 large egg whites
2 teaspoons vegetable oil
10 ounces fresh mushrooms, sliced
1 medium onion, finely chopped
1 carrot, finely chopped
1 celery rib, finely chopped
1 garlic clove, minced
1 teaspoon dried thyme
½ teaspoon salt
¼ teaspoon freshly ground black pepper
2 cups chicken stock, preferably homemade (page 212), or
  low-sodium canned broth, heated to boiling
1 cup dried farfalle (bow tie pasta)
¼ cup chopped fresh parsley

―――

1. In a large nonstick skillet, combine the kasha and egg substitute, and cook over medium heat, stirring constantly, until the egg is set and lightly browned, about 3 minutes. Transfer to a bowl and set aside.

2. Return the skillet to medium heat and add the oil. Add the mushrooms, onion, carrot, celery, and garlic, cover, and cook until the mushrooms have released their juices, about 5 minutes. Uncover and continue to cook until the juices have evaporated, 3 to 5 minutes.

3. Return the kasha to the pan, and add the thyme, salt, and pepper. Pour in the boiling stock, reduce the heat to low, cover, and cook until all the liquid has been absorbed, 12 to 15 minutes.

4. Meanwhile, in a large pot of boiling salted water, cook the pasta until just tender, about 9 minutes. Drain and return to the pot.

5. Fluff the kasha with a fork and add to the pasta. Toss well, transfer to a warmed serving bowl, and sprinkle with the parsley. Serve immediately.

Note: Many bow tie–shaped pastas are made with egg yolks. To be sure you are getting egg-free pasta, buy an imported Italian variety, most of which are made with only durum semolina and water (labeled *farfalle*).

NUTRITIONAL ANALYSIS PER SERVING (BASED ON 8 SERVINGS)
CALORIES: 544 (12 percent from protein, 83 percent from carbohydrate, 5 percent from fat) •
PROTEIN: 16 grams • CARBOHYDRATE: 107 grams • FAT: 3 grams • CHOLESTEROL: 0 milligrams
• SODIUM: 333 milligrams

SPAGHETTI WITH TOMATO-VODKA SAUCE

MAKES 6 TO 8 SERVINGS

―――

Over the last decade, this brightly flavored dish has shown up on more and more restaurant menus, to the point that it can now be called a classic. Even though you may not perceive the vodka in the sauce, don't leave it out—it really heightens the flavor.

―――

(continued)

3 garlic cloves, chopped
2 teaspoons olive oil
1 28-ounce can crushed tomatoes in puree
1 cup evaporated skimmed milk
½ teaspoon crushed hot red pepper
1 pound dried spaghetti
2 tablespoons vodka
¼ cup chopped fresh basil or parsley

———

1. In a medium saucepan, cook the garlic in the oil over medium-low heat, stirring constantly, until lightly browned, 2 minutes. Add the tomatoes, increase the heat to medium, and bring to a simmer. Cook until the juices are slightly reduced and the sauce has thickened, 15 to 20 minutes.

2. Stir in the skimmed milk and hot pepper, bring to a simmer, lower the heat, and cook for 5 minutes.

3. Meanwhile, in a large pot of boiling salted water, cook the pasta, until barely tender, about 7 minutes. Drain and return to the pot.

4. Stir the vodka into the hot tomato sauce, and add to the pasta. Toss well, transfer to a warmed serving bowl, and sprinkle with the chopped basil. Serve immediately.

NUTRITIONAL ANALYSIS PER SERVING (BASED ON 8 SERVINGS)

CALORIES: 300 (15 percent from protein, 76 percent from carbohydrate, 7 percent from fat) • PROTEIN: 11 grams • CARBOHYDRATE: 56 grams • FAT: 2 grams • CHOLESTEROL: 1 milligram • SODIUM: 286 milligrams

Pasta al Forno

❖

As a dinner party host, I have done it all. I've flambéed crêpes, my guests gasping (with appreciation and terror) as I've sent blue flames shooting up into the air. I've taken days to bone, marinate, stuff, poach, chill, and sauce turkeys, changing a humble bird into a luxurious galantine. I've even rubbed edible gold onto a marzipan-wrapped cake until it looked like a burnished, gilded jewel box. But, nothing, *nothing* is as surefire a crowd pleaser as bringing a bubbling, steaming, crusty dish of baked pasta to the table.

Maybe it's nostalgia for Mom's casseroles. Even though they weren't culinary wonders, they were warming, filling, and comforting. But they were never low-fat. What's wonderful about these recipes is that they are warming, filling, comforting, *and* low-fat. You'll find a large range of possibilities here, from company dishes such as Shellfish and Mushroom Lasagne, to everyday fare the whole family will love, like Inside-Out Ravioli Bake.

Dried pastas hold up better to saucing and baking than fresh. Remember that the pasta will cook further as it bakes in the oven, so don't boil it too long—taste frequently and boil only until it is barely tender.

GREEK LAMB AND ZUCCHINI PASTICCIO

MAKES 6 TO 8 SERVINGS

———

A seemingly familiar tomato-sauced pasta casserole is made extraordinary with the traditional Greek touches of ground cinnamon and lamb and the addition of a simple yogurt topping. Ground lamb isn't carried by every butcher, and when you do find it, it can be quite fatty. I prefer to buy cubes of lean, boneless leg of lamb (like shish kebab), trim them well, and grind them in my food processor.

———

Nonstick vegetable cooking spray
12 ounces boneless leg of lamb cut into 1-inch cubes, well trimmed
2 teaspoons olive oil
1 medium onion, chopped
2 garlic cloves, minced
2 medium zucchini, well scrubbed, halved lengthwise, and
  cut into ½-inch-thick half-moons
1 28-ounce can tomatoes in puree
1 8-ounce can tomato sauce
¾ cup red wine
2 teaspoons dried oregano
1 teaspoon ground cinnamon
¼ teaspoon freshly ground black pepper
1 pound dried tubular pasta, such as penne
1 cup plain nonfat yogurt
½ cup liquid egg substitute or 4 egg whites

———

1. Place the lamb in the freezer until partially frozen, about 30 minutes. Transfer to a food processor fitted with the metal blade, and process the lamb until coarsely ground.

2. Preheat the oven to 350°F. Lightly spray a 2½-quart round casserole with nonstick cooking spray.

3. In a large saucepan, heat the oil over medium-high heat. Add the ground lamb and cook, stirring often, until it loses its pink color, about 5 minutes. Add the onion and garlic and cook until the onion is softened, about 2 minutes. Add the zucchini and cook for 2 minutes. Stir in the tomatoes with their puree, the tomato sauce, red wine, oregano, cinnamon, and pepper. Bring to a simmer, reduce the heat to low, cover, and simmer, stirring occasionally, until the sauce is slightly thickened, about 45 minutes.

4. Meanwhile, in a large pot of boiling salted water, cook the pasta until barely tender, about 7 minutes. (Do not overcook; the pasta will cook further in the oven.) Drain well, and return to the pot.

5. Add the lamb sauce to the pasta and mix well. Transfer to the prepared baking dish.

6. In a small bowl, stir together the yogurt and egg substitute. Pour evenly over the top of the pasta. Bake until the top is golden brown, 30 to 40 minutes. Let stand for 5 minutes before serving.

NUTRITIONAL ANALYSIS PER SERVING (BASED ON 8 SERVINGS)

CALORIES: 402 (22 percent from protein, 62 percent from carbohydrate, 12 percent from fat) • PROTEIN: 22 grams • CARBOHYDRATE: 62 grams • FAT: 5 grams • CHOLESTEROL: 29 milligrams • SODIUM: 508 milligrams

CHEESY VEGETABLE AND PASTA BAKE

MAKES 6 TO 8 SERVINGS

I like to think of this as upscale macaroni and cheese. What I really like about it is the crunchy top of the baked pasta. I created this from the vegetables left over in the refrigerator after a couple of days of cooking; feel free to mix and match ingredients from your kitchen.

Nonstick vegetable cooking spray
1 pound dried tubular pasta, such as penne
1 medium onion, chopped
1 medium red bell pepper, stemmed, seeded, and chopped
1 medium zucchini, well scrubbed, halved lengthwise, and
  cut into ¼-inch-thick half-moons
8 ounces fresh mushrooms, sliced
2 garlic cloves, minced
2 cups (16 ounces) nonfat cottage or ricotta cheese
¾ cup evaporated skimmed milk
½ cup liquid egg substitute or 4 large egg whites
4 ripe medium plum tomatoes, chopped
1 10-ounce package frozen chopped spinach, defrosted and
  squeezed dry
½ cup chopped fresh basil
½ teaspoon salt
¼ teaspoon freshly ground black pepper
1 cup shredded nonfat mozzarella cheese (4 ounces)

---

1. Preheat the oven to 350°F. Lightly spray a 13- by 9-inch baking dish with nonstick vegetable spray.

2. In a large pot of boiling salted water, cook the pasta until just tender, about 7 minutes. (Do not overcook; the pasta will cook further in the oven.) Drain, rinse under cold water, drain well, and return to the pot.

3. Meanwhile, spray a large nonstick skillet with nonstick vegetable spray and heat over medium heat. Add the onion, red pepper, zucchini, mushrooms, and garlic and cook, covered, until the onions are softened and the mushrooms have released their liquid, about 5 minutes. Uncover and cook until all the liquid has evaporated, about 3 minutes.

4. Stir the vegetable mixture into the pasta.

5. In a food processor or blender, process the cottage cheese, evaporated skimmed milk, and egg substitute until smooth. Pour over the pasta. Add the tomatoes, spinach, and basil and mix well. Transfer the pasta to the prepared dish, and sprinkle with the mozzarella cheese. Bake until golden brown on top, 25 to 35 minutes. Let stand for 5 minutes before serving.

NUTRITIONAL ANALYSIS PER SERVING (BASED ON 8 SERVINGS)

CALORIES: 356 (29 percent from protein, 66 percent from carbohydrate, 5 percent from fat) • PROTEIN: 26 grams • CARBOHYDRATE: 60 grams • FAT: 2 grams • CHOLESTEROL: 6 milligrams • SODIUM: 317 milligrams

---

UPDATED CHILI MAC

Another down-home casserole that gets a makeover with lean ground turkey. The addition of black beans to the pasta increases the protein content of the dish.

-----

1 *pound ground turkey*
1 *medium onion, chopped*
1 *garlic clove, minced*
1 *28-ounce can tomatoes in juice*
1½ *cups (12 ounces) canned tomato puree*
1 *tablespoon chili powder, or more to taste*
1 *16-ounce can black beans, drained and rinsed*
1 *cup fresh or defrosted frozen corn kernels*
1 *teaspoon salt*
¾ *pound dried elbow macaroni*
¾ *cup shredded reduced-fat Cheddar cheese (3 ounces)*

-----

1. Preheat the oven to 350°F. Lightly spray a deep 2½-quart baking dish with nonstick vegetable spray.

2. Lightly spray a medium saucepan with cooking spray. Add the turkey, onion, and garlic, and cook over medium heat, stirring occasionally with a wooden spoon to break up the meat, until the turkey loses its pink color, about 5 minutes. Drain off any juices.

3. Add the tomatoes, tomato puree, and chili powder. Bring to a simmer and cook, stirring occasionally, for 5 minutes. Stir in the beans, corn, and salt and simmer until the sauce is slightly thickened, about 5 minutes.

4. Meanwhile, in a large pot of boiling salted water, cook the pasta until barely tender, about 6 minutes. (Do not overcook; the pasta will cook further in the oven.) Drain well, and return to the pot.

5. Add the chili mixture to the pasta and toss well. Spoon into the prepared baking dish and sprinkle with the grated cheese. Bake until bubbling and heated through, about 25 minutes. Let stand 5 minutes before serving.

NUTRITIONAL ANALYSIS PER SERVING (BASED ON 8 SERVINGS)

CALORIES: 365 (23 percent from protein, 59 percent from carbohydrate, 19 percent from fat) • PROTEIN: 22 grams • CARBOHYDRATE: 56 grams • FAT: 8 grams • CHOLESTEROL: 29 milligrams • SODIUM: 742 milligrams

SPINACH PASTA "PIE"

———

This is an impressive-looking, vibrantly colored dish. As it is free-standing and easy to slice, I like to bring it to the table on a cake stand. Served hot with a spoonful of tomato sauce, it is a nice brunch or supper dish; it can also be served at room temperature, making it perfect for buffets and picnics.

———

Nonstick vegetable cooking spray
12 ounces dried spinach fettuccine
2 teaspoons olive oil
1 medium onion, chopped
1 medium red bell pepper, stemmed, seeded, and chopped
2 garlic cloves, minced
2 10-ounce packages frozen chopped spinach, thawed and
  squeezed dry
1½ cups reduced-fat ricotta cheese
¾ cup liquid egg substitute
1 teaspoon dried basil
1 teaspoon dried oregano
½ teaspoon salt
¼ teaspoon freshly ground black pepper
2 cups Herbed Marinara Sauce (page 90), warmed (optional)

———

1. Preheat the oven to 350°F. Lightly spray a 9-inch springform pan with nonstick cooking spray.

2. In a large pot of boiling salted water, cook the pasta until barely tender, about 6 minutes. Drain, rinse under cold water, and drain well.

3. Meanwhile, in a medium nonstick skillet, heat the oil over medium-low heat. Add the onion, red pepper, and garlic and cook, stirring often, until the onions are golden, about 5 minutes. Remove from the heat.

4. In a large mixing bowl, combine the spinach, cooked vegetables, ricotta, egg substitute, basil, oregano, salt, and pepper and mix well. Add the drained pasta and mix well. Spoon the mixture into the prepared pan, pressing down lightly with the back of a spoon. Cover with aluminum foil, and bake for 20 minutes. Uncover and continue to bake until the pie is set in the center and lightly golden on top, about 40 minutes.

5. Run a knife around the inside of the pan to release the pie. Let stand for 5 minutes before removing the springform sides. Serve hot with the tomato sauce, or at room temperature without sauce.

NUTRITIONAL ANALYSIS PER SERVING (BASED ON 8 SERVINGS)

CALORIES: 252 (23 percent from protein, 57 percent from carbohydrate, 20 percent from fat) • PROTEIN: 15 grams • CARBOHYDRATE: 38 grams • FAT: 6 grams • CHOLESTEROL: 42 milligrams • SODIUM: 329 milligrams

TURKEY AND BROCCOLI MANICOTTI WITH RED PEPPER–TOMATO CREAM

MAKES 8 SERVINGS

Manicotti is perfect for serving a crowd. This is an upscale, low-fat version of the traditional baked dish. Freshly roasted peppers are best, but you can substitute two seven-ounce jars of roasted red peppers in a pinch.

RED PEPPER–TOMATO CREAM

4 medium red bell peppers
1 16-ounce can tomatoes, in juice, drained
2¾ cups nonfat ricotta cheese
*½ cup chicken stock, preferably homemade (page 212), or low-
  sodium canned broth*
1 garlic clove, minced
¼ teaspoon salt
¼ teaspoon freshly ground black pepper

TURKEY-BROCCOLI FILLING

2 cups finely chopped broccoli (stems and florets)
12 ounces ground turkey
1 medium onion, chopped
1 medium red bell pepper, stemmed, seeded, and chopped
1 garlic clove, minced
½ teaspoon dried thyme
½ teaspoon dried marjoram
½ teaspoon salt
¼ teaspoon freshly ground black pepper
1¼ cups nonfat ricotta cheese

Nonstick vegetable cooking spray
16 dried manicotti tubes (8 ounces)
⅓ cup freshly grated imported Parmesan cheese

----

1. Preheat the oven to 500°F.

2. Make the red pepper cream: Place the red peppers on a baking sheet and roast, turning occasionally, until the skins are charred and blistered, about 30 minutes. Transfer to a bag, close, and let stand 20 minutes. Reduce the oven temperature to 350°F.

3. Remove and discard the stems, skins, and seeds from the roasted peppers. Transfer the peppers to a blender and add the tomatoes, ricotta, chicken stock, garlic, salt, and pepper. Process until smooth. Set aside.

4. Make the filling: In a large saucepan of boiling lightly salted water, cook the broccoli until crisp-tender, about 3 minutes. Drain, rinse under cold water, and drain well.

5. In a large nonstick skillet, combine the turkey, onion, red pepper, garlic, thyme, marjoram, salt, and pepper. Cook over medium-high heat, breaking up the turkey with a wooden spoon, until the turkey loses its pink color, about 5 minutes. Drain off any liquid, and cool completely. Then stir in the chopped broccoli and the ricotta.

6. Meanwhile, in a large pot of boiling salted water, cook the pasta until barely tender, about 6 minutes. (Do not overcook; the pasta will cook further in the oven.) Drain, rinse under cold water, and drain again.

7. Lightly spray a 15- by 10-inch baking dish with nonstick vegetable spray. Spread a thin layer of the red pepper cream over the bottom of the dish. Stuff the manicotti tubes with the turkey-broccoli filling, and arrange in a single layer in the pan. Spread the remaining red pepper cream over the manicotti, and sprinkle with the Parmesan cheese.

8. Cover with aluminum foil and bake for 20 minutes. Uncover and continue baking until bubbling and heated through, about 10 minutes longer. Let stand 5 minutes before serving.

NUTRITIONAL ANALYSIS PER SERVING

CALORIES: 318 (38 percent from protein, 47 percent from carbohydrate, 15 percent from fat) • PROTEIN: 31 grams • CARBOHYDRATE: 38 grams • FAT: 5 grams • CHOLESTEROL: 39 milligrams • SODIUM: 712 milligrams

SHELLFISH AND MUSHROOM LASAGNE

MAKES 9 SERVINGS

     —

Every caterer has a "secret weapon"—a surefire winner of a dish that is guaranteed to win comments of appreciation, not to mention clients. This delectable, low-fat seafood lasagne was mine. Everyone loves lasagne, but not the calories and fat that come with the typical beef version. Here two sauces—creamy white wine and herbed tomato—blend with shellfish to make a truly special entrée. I know this recipe looks long, but I have written particularly detailed instructions based on my years of perfecting it.

     —

SHELLFISH FILLING

Nonstick vegetable cooking spray
1½ pounds fresh mushrooms, sliced
3 shallots, minced
1½ pounds bay scallops
1½ pounds medium shrimp, peeled and deveined
½ cup dry white wine or dry vermouth
¼ teaspoon salt, plus more to taste
¼ teaspoon freshly ground black pepper
3 cups nonfat ricotta cheese
¼ cup chopped fresh parsley

1 pound freshly made pasta dough
3 cups Herbed Marinara Sauce (page 90), pulsed in a food
    processor until fairly smooth
⅓ cup freshly grated imported Parmesan cheese

     —

1. Spray a large nonstick skillet with nonstick vegetable spray. Add the mushrooms and shallots and cook, covered, over medium heat, until the mushrooms release their liquid, about 5 minutes. Uncover and cook, stirring occasionally until all the liquid has evaporated and the mushrooms are browned, about 5 minutes. Transfer to a medium bowl.

2. Add the scallops, shrimp, wine, salt, and pepper to the skillet. Bring to a simmer over medium heat and cook, stirring often, just until the shrimp are pink and the scallops are opaque, about 2 minutes. Be careful not to overcook the shellfish. Place in a large colander set over a bowl and drain for 10 minutes. Reserve the cooking liquid; coarsely chop the shellfish and add to the mushrooms.

3. Return the reserved cooking liquid to the skillet, bring to a boil over high heat, and cook until reduced to ⅓ cup, about 5 minutes. Transfer to a blender, add the ricotta cheese, and process until smooth. Pour over the shellfish-mushroom mixture, add the parsley, and mix well.

4. Preheat the oven to 350°F. Lightly spray a 13- by 9-inch baking dish with nonstick vegetable spray.

5. A little organization will make the next steps go smoothly: Bring a large pot of water to a boil over high heat. (A pasta pot with a perforated insert for draining works best. Or use a large skimmer to remove the pasta from its cooking water.) Add salt to taste, and reduce the heat to medium-low to maintain a steady simmer. Set a large bowl of cold water next to your stove, and lay out a clean kitchen towel near your sink. Place the shellfish filling and marinara sauce on your work surface.

6. Cut the pasta dough into six portions. Roll out each portion to a ¹⁄₁₆ inch thick (Number 5 setting on most hand-cranked pasta machines). Let dry slightly until moist, but still supple, about 10 minutes. Cut the pasta sheets into 13-inch strips, reserving any end pieces for patching, if necessary. (The exact number of lasagne noodles and their width will depend on your pasta machine; pasta from an electric extruder will be narrower and thicker than that from a hand-cranked machine. Any leftover sheets can be cut into fettuccine for another dish.) You will need 2 to 4 strips of lasagne per layer, for a total of four layers. Don't let the pasta dry until it's brittle—proceed immediately.

7. Work with only enough pasta strips for one layer at a time. Cook the lasagne in the simmering water until barely softened, about 15 seconds. (Do not overcook; the lasagne will cook further in the oven.) Using the perforated insert, drain the lasagne (or carefully remove the lasagne from the water with the large skimmer), and transfer to the bowl of cold water. Bring the bowl to your sink. Lift out, rinse and unfold the lasagne carefully under gently running water, then lay the lasagne on the kitchen towel, and pat dry.

(continued)

8. Spread a thin layer of the marinara sauce over the bottom of the prepared dish. Lay the lasagne in the dish, overlapping it, and spread with one third of the seafood filling. Cook another batch of lasagne strips, drain, rinse, and pat dry. Place in the pan and cover with half of the remaining filling. Cooking another batch of lasagne and place in the pan. Cover with the remaining filling. Cook a final batch of lasagne, and place in the pan. Spread with the remaining tomato sauce, then sprinkle with the Parmesan cheese. Cover with aluminum foil. (The lasagna can be prepared up to 4 hours ahead and refrigerated. Let stand at room temperature for 30 minutes before baking.)

9. Bake the lasagne for 30 minutes. Remove the foil and continue baking until bubbling and heated through, about 15 more minutes. Let the lasagne stand for 10 minutes before serving.

Note: An alternative to making your own pasta for lasagne is to buy sheets of fresh pasta from an Italian specialty grocer and cut them into the desired lengths. Yes, you can substitute dried lasagne: Use 12 strips of pasta (9 ounces), and cook in boiling salted water until barely tender, about 7 minutes. Because dried lasagne is thicker than fresh, the layering is different: a thin layer of sauce, then a layer of noodles, half of the filling, a layer of pasta, the remaining filling, another layer of pasta, and the remaining tomato sauce and Parmesan.

NUTRITIONAL ANALYSIS PER SERVING

CALORIES: 448 (44 percent from protein, 45 percent from carbohydrate, 11 percent from fat) • PROTEIN: 49 grams • CARBOHYDRATE: 51 grams • FAT: 5 grams • CHOLESTEROL: 201 milligrams • SODIUM: 648 milligrams

MEXICAN MANICOTTI

Italian meets Mexican in this fun-to-make (and eat) entrée. The dish can be assembled up to six hours ahead before baking, provided it is covered and refrigerated.

ZUCCHINI AND CORN FILLING

Nonstick vegetable cooking spray
2 medium zucchini, well scrubbed and finely chopped
1 medium onion, finely chopped
1 medium red bell pepper, stemmed, seeded, and finely chopped
1 garlic clove, minced
1 tablespoon olive oil
1½ cups fresh or defrosted frozen corn kernels
1 tablespoon dried oregano
1 teaspoon chili powder
½ teaspoon ground cumin
½ teaspoon salt
1 cup nonfat ricotta cheese
½ cup fresh bread crumbs
¼ cup liquid egg substitute or 2 large egg whites

SPICY TOMATO SAUCE

2 28-ounce cans tomatoes in juice, drained
1 medium onion, quartered
1 garlic clove, crushed
1 fresh hot chile pepper, such as jalepeño, seeded and minced
1 tablespoon olive oil

8 ounces dried manicotti

---

1. Preheat the oven to 350°F. Spray a 13- by 9-inch baking dish with nonstick vegetable spray.

(continued)

2. Make the filling: In a large nonstick skillet, cook the zucchini, onion, bell pepper, and garlic in the oil over medium heat, covered, stirring often, until the vegetables are softened, about 5 minutes. Stir in the corn, oregano, chili powder, cumin, and salt, increase the heat to medium-high, and cook, stirring, until the liquid given off by the vegetables is evaporated about 5 minutes. Transfer to a medium bowl and let cool completely, then stir in the ricotta, bread crumbs, and egg substitute. Set aside.

3. Make the sauce: In a blender or a food processor fitted with the metal blade, process the tomatoes, onion, chile pepper, and garlic until smooth.

4. In a large nonstick skillet, heat the oil over medium-high heat. Add the pureed tomatoes and cook, stirring often, until the sauce has thickened slightly, about 4 minutes. Remove from the heat.

5. In a large pot of boiling salted water, cook the pasta until barely tender, about 6 minutes. (Do not overcook; the pasta will cook further in the oven.) Drain, rinse carefully under cold water, and drain well.

6. Spread a thin layer of the tomato sauce over the bottom of the prepared dish. Stuff the manicotti tubes with the vegetable-ricotta filling, and arrange in a single layer in the baking dish. Spread the remaining sauce over the manicotti. Cover with aluminum foil.

7. Bake for 20 minutes. Remove the foil and bake until the manicotti is heated through, about 20 more minutes. Let stand 5 minutes before serving.

NUTRITIONAL ANALYSIS PER SERVING

CALORIES: 273 (18 percent from protein, 66 percent from carbohydrate, 16 percent from fat) • PROTEIN: 13 grams • CARBOHYDRATE: 47 grams • FAT: 5 grams • CHOLESTEROL: 5 milligrams • SODIUM: 531 milligrams

SHRIMP-AND-SPINACH-STUFFED SHELLS

These have become favorite company fare at my house, as everyone, especially my guests' kids, loves them.

Nonstick vegetable cooking spray
1 pound medium shrimp
2 10-ounce packages frozen chopped spinach, defrosted and
  squeezed dry
2 cups nonfat ricotta cheese
½ cup liquid egg substitute or 4 large egg whites
⅔ cup fresh bread crumbs
1½ teaspoons dried rosemary
½ teaspoon salt
¼ teaspoon freshly ground black pepper
⅛ teaspoon grated nutmeg
24 dried jumbo pasta shells (12 ounces)
5 cups Herbed Marinara Sauce (page 90)

1. Preheat the oven to 350°F. Lightly spray a 13- by 9-inch baking dish with nonstick vegetable spray.

2. In a medium saucepan of boiling salted water, cook the shrimp just until pink and firm, about 3 minutes. Drain, transfer to a bowl of cold water to cool quickly, and drain again.

3. Peel and devein the shrimp, then coarsely chop. Transfer to a large bowl. Add the spinach, ricotta, egg substitute, bread crumbs, rosemary, salt, pepper, and nutmeg and mix well. Set aside.

4. In a large pot of boiling salted water, cook the pasta until just tender, about 6 minutes. (Do not overcook; the pasta will cook further in the oven.) Drain, rinse carefully under cold water, and drain well.

5. Spread 2 cups of the tomato sauce over the bottom of the prepared dish. Stuff the shells with the filling and place in a single layer in the

dish. Spread the remaining sauce over the shells, and cover with aluminum foil.

6. Bake the shells for 15 minutes. Uncover and continue baking until the shells are heated through, about 15 minutes longer. Let stand 5 minutes.

NUTRITIONAL ANALYSIS PER SERVING

CALORIES: 362 (32 percent from protein, 58 percent from carbohydrate, 10 percent from fat) • PROTEIN: 30 grams • CARBOHYDRATE: 54 grams • FAT: 4 grams • CHOLESTEROL: 97 milligrams • SODIUM: 615 milligrams

---

INSIDE-OUT RAVIOLI BAKE

MAKES 6 SERVINGS

———

An old-time favorite that gets an update with ground turkey and nonfat cheeses.

———

Nonstick vegetable cooking spray
1 pound ground turkey
1 medium onion, chopped
1 garlic clove, minced
1 28-ounce can crushed tomatoes in puree
1 8-ounce can tomato sauce
1 teaspoon dried basil
1 teaspoon dried oregano
¼ teaspoon freshly ground black pepper
1 10-ounce package frozen spinach, defrosted and squeezed dry
1 cup nonfat ricotta cheese
½ cup liquid egg substitute or 2 large egg whites
8 ounces dried farfalle (bow tie pasta)
⅓ cup freshly grated imported Parmesan cheese

———

1. Preheat the oven to 350°F. Lightly spray a 2-quart round casserole with nonstick cooking spray.

2. In a large nonstick skillet, combine the turkey, onion, and garlic and cook over medium heat, stirring with a spoon to break up the turkey, until the turkey loses its pink color, about 5 minutes. Drain off any liquid. Stir in the tomatoes, tomato sauce, basil, oregano, and pepper and bring to a simmer. Reduce the heat to low, and cook for 5 minutes.

3. Meanwhile, in a large pot of boiling salted water, cook the pasta until barely tender, about 6 minutes. (Do not overcook; the pasta will cook further in the oven.) Drain and return to the pot.

4. Add the tomato mixture to the pasta and toss well. Stir in the spinach, ricotta cheese, and egg substitute. Transfer to the prepared dish and sprinkle with the Parmesan cheese. Bake until bubbling and heated through, about 30 minutes. Let stand 5 minutes before serving.

NUTRITIONAL ANALYSIS PER SERVING

CALORIES: 394 (29 percent from protein, 50 percent from carbohydrate, 20 percent from fat) • PROTEIN: 29 grams • CARBOHYDRATE: 50 grams • FAT: 9 grams • CHOLESTEROL: 39 milligrams • SODIUM: 858 milligrams

TODAY'S TURKEY TETRAZZINI

MAKES 6 TO 8 SERVINGS

I wonder how many casseroles of turkey tetrazzini are whipped up the day after Thanksgiving? I love this dish as much as the next person (maybe more), but if you're like me, the last thing you need to make with leftover holiday turkey is something high in calories. Here is a low-fat version for tetrazzini lovers everywhere.

1 pound dried spaghetti
Nonstick vegetable cooking spray
1 9-ounce package frozen artichoke hearts, defrosted and
*   coarsely chopped*
8 ounces fresh mushrooms, sliced
⅓ cup dry sherry
⅓ cup chopped fresh parsley
3 shallots or scallions, chopped
1 garlic clove, minced
1 teaspoon dried tarragon
½ teaspoon salt
¼ teaspoon freshly ground black pepper
2 cups nonfat ricotta cheese
1 cup skim milk
2 cups cubed (¾-inch) cooked turkey breast (about 10 ounces)
½ cup fresh bread crumbs

1. Preheat the oven to 350°F. Lightly spray a 13- by 9-inch baking dish with nonstick vegetable spray.

2. In a large pot of boiling salted water, cook the pasta until barely tender, about 7 minutes. (Do not overcook; the pasta will cook further in the oven.) Drain, rinse under cold water, drain well, and return to the pot.

3. Meanwhile, spray a large nonstick skillet with cooking spray and heat over medium heat. Add the artichokes, mushrooms, sherry, parsley, shallots, garlic, tarragon, salt, and pepper. Cook, stirring occasionally, until the mushrooms have softened, about 5 minutes.

4. Add the vegetables to the pasta, then add the ricotta, skim milk, and turkey, and mix well. Spread evenly in the prepared dish. Sprinkle with the bread crumbs.

5. Bake until the top is golden brown, 30 to 40 minutes. Let stand 5 minutes before serving.

NUTRITIONAL ANALYSIS PER SERVING (BASED ON 8 SERVINGS)

CALORIES: 385 (33 percent from protein, 58 percent from carbohydrate, 6 percent from fat) • PROTEIN: 32 grams • CARBOHYDRATE: 56 grams • FAT: 3 grams • CHOLESTEROL: 42 milligrams • SODIUM: 379 milligrams

---

Dinner in the Time
It Takes the Water
to Boil

Pasta may now be recognized as a healthful food, but I know darned well that there was another reason for its renaissance a few years back— it is fast and easy to cook! In our haste, our pasta dishes were not always as nutritious as they could have been. The pasta was healthful, but what we put on it was not.

These recipes combine health with speed and ease of preparation. All of them can be prepared in the fifteen to twenty minutes it takes the pasta water to come to a boil. And if you make the dish with store-bought fresh pasta, you'll really have dinner in record time.

Pasta should be sauced as soon as it is drained. Time the sauce so it is ready at the same time as the pasta. Or, more realistically, rest assured that none of these sauces will suffer if they are finished a bit ahead of time and are kept warm on the stove until the pasta is cooked and ready to be tossed.

SPICY CAJUN SHRIMP ON LINGUINE

MAKES 6 TO 8 SERVINGS

W̲ith a little bit of this and a little bit of that, you can create taste-tingling Cajun seasoning to spice up a shrimp sauté. And by using stewed tomatoes that have already been cooked with onions, sweet peppers, and celery, you'll bring this dish across the finish line in record time. If you make your own pasta, try Spicy Cajun Pasta on page 55.

1 teaspoon sweet Hungarian paprika
1 teaspoon dried basil
1 teaspoon dried thyme
⅛ teaspoon cayenne pepper
2 teaspoons olive oil
1 pound medium shrimp, peeled and deveined
2 scallions, chopped
2 garlic cloves, minced
2 14½-ounce cans stewed tomatoes with onion, celery, and
   green pepper, drained
Hot red pepper sauce to taste
1 pound freshly made or store-bought fresh cholesterol-free linguine

1. In a medium bowl, combine the paprika, basil, thyme, and cayenne pepper.

2. In a large nonstick skillet, heat the oil over medium heat. Add the shrimp and cook, stirring often, just until pink and firm, 2 to 3 minutes. Using a slotted spoon, transfer the shrimp to the bowl of seasonings. Toss well to coat, and set aside.

3. Add the scallions and garlic to the skillet and cook over medium heat until softened, about 1 minute. Add the stewed tomatoes and bring to a simmer. Reduce the heat to low, cover, and cook for 5 minutes. Stir in the shrimp and hot pepper sauce. Keep warm.

4. Meanwhile, in a large pot of boiling salted water, cook the pasta until just tender, 1 to 2 minutes. Drain and return to the pot.

5. Add the sauce and toss well. Transfer to a warmed serving bowl and serve immediately.

NUTRITIONAL ANALYSIS PER SERVING (BASED ON 8 SERVINGS)

CALORIES: 254 (26 percent from protein, 61 percent from carbohydrate, 13 percent from fat) • **PROTEIN:** 16 grams • **CARBOHYDRATE:** 38 grams • **FAT:** 4 grams • **CHOLESTEROL:** 87 milligrams • **SODIUM:** 342 milligrams

SICILIAN TUNA AND TOMATO PASTA

MAKES 6 TO 8 SERVINGS

There are few dishes with a more colorful history than this lusty pasta. Legend has it that when a Sicilian prostitute needed a quick bite between assignations, she would slap together this bold sauce of tomatoes, anchovies, and garlic to dress her spaghetti. I always add a can of tuna to my sauce for more sustenance.

8 anchovy fillets in olive oil, drained (reserve 2 teaspoons of the anchovy oil), rinsed, and finely chopped

2 garlic cloves, minced

1 28-ounce can crushed tomatoes in puree

12 Mediterranean black olives, pitted and chopped

1 tablespoon capers, rinsed

2 teaspoons dried oregano

¼ teaspoon crushed hot red pepper

1 6¼-ounce can tuna packed in water, drained and flaked

1 pound dried spaghetti

1. In a medium skillet, combine the anchovies, garlic and the reserved 2 teaspoons anchovy oil and stir over medium heat until the garlic is softened, about 1 minute. Stir in the tomatoes, olives, capers, oregano, and crushed red pepper. Bring to a simmer and cook briskly until the sauce has thickened slightly, about 5 minutes. Stir in the tuna and cook for 1 minute. Keep warm.

2. Meanwhile, in a large pot of boiling salted water, cook the pasta until just tender, about 7 minutes. Drain and return to the pot.

3. Add the tomato sauce and toss well. Transfer to a warmed serving bowl and serve immediately.

NUTRITIONAL ANALYSIS PER SERVING (BASED ON 8 SERVINGS)

CALORIES: 323 (20 percent from protein, 63 percent from carbohydrate, 17 percent from fat) • PROTEIN: 16 grams • CARBOHYDRATE: 51 grams • FAT: 6 grams • CHOLESTEROL: 13 milligrams • SODIUM: 659 milligrams

FETTUCCINE WITH MADRAS CHICKEN YOGURT SAUCE

———

Here's a spicy blend of Indian and Italian cuisines. While I created this sauce specifically for Curry Pasta (page 52), it can be served on plain store-bought fettuccine if the amount of curry powder is increased to one tablespoon.

———

1 *pound boneless, skinless chicken cutlets, cut into strips*
   2 inches long by ½ inch thick
2 *tablespoons all-purpose flour*
2 *teaspoons vegetable oil*
1 *medium onion, chopped*
1 *medium Granny Smith apple, peeled, cored, and chopped*
1 *celery rib, chopped*
1 *garlic clove, minced*
1 *cup plus 2 tablespoons chicken stock, preferably homemade*
   (page 212), or low-sodium canned broth
1 *teaspoon curry powder, preferably Madras-style*
½ *teaspoon salt*
⅓ *cup raisins*
1 *pound freshly made or store-bought fresh cholesterol-free*
   fettuccine
¾ *cup plain nonfat yogurt*
1 *scallion, chopped*

———

1. In a medium bowl, toss the chicken strips with the flour.

2. In a large nonstick skillet, heat the oil over medium-high heat. Add the chicken and cook, turning occasionally, until lightly browned on all sides, about 3 minutes. Transfer to a plate and set aside.

(continued)

3. Add the onion, apple, celery, and garlic to the skillet and stir for 1 minute. Add 2 tablespoons of the chicken stock, reduce the heat to medium, cover, and cook until the vegetables are softened, about 5 minutes. Sprinkle with the curry powder and salt and stir for 1 minute.

4. Return the chicken strips to the skillet. Add the raisins and the remaining 1 cup stock and stir well. Bring to a simmer and cook until the sauce has thickened slightly, about 3 minutes. Remove from the heat and keep warm.

5. In a large pot of boiling salted water, cook the pasta until just tender, 2 to 3 minutes. Drain well and return to the pot.

6. Stir ·the yogurt into the sauce and stir over low heat until heated through, about 1 minute; do not boil. Add the sauce to the pasta and toss well. Transfer to a warmed serving bowl and serve immediately, sprinkling each serving with chopped scallion.

NUTRITIONAL ANALYSIS PER SERVING (BASED ON 8 SERVINGS)

CALORIES: 290 (23 percent from protein, 63 percent from carbohydrate, 14 percent from fat) • PROTEIN: 17 grams • CARBOHYDRATE: 45 grams • FAT: 4 grams • CHOLESTEROL: 23 milligrams • SODIUM: 290 milligrams

FETTUCCINE WITH CRAB HASH

Lump crabmeat in a highly seasoned, creamy sauce is one of the glories of Chesapeake Bay cooking, and this trimmed-down version is equally glorious. While I like to serve this on Maryland Spice Box Pasta (page 56), you can certainly make do with plain fresh fettuccine; just increase the Old Bay Seasoning in the hash by half a teaspoon.

Nonstick vegetable cooking spray
1/2 cup finely chopped red pepper
2 scallions, chopped
1 celery rib, chopped
4 plum tomatoes, seeded and chopped
1 fresh hot chile pepper, such as jalepeño, seeded and minced
1 pound lump crabmeat, picked over for shells and cartilage
1/2 cup evaporated skimmed milk
1/2 cup bottled clam juice
3/4 teaspoon Old Bay Seasoning
1 pound freshly made or store-bought fresh cholesterol-free
*   fettuccine*
Salt to taste

1. Lightly spray a medium nonstick skillet with nonstick cooking spray and heat over medium heat. Add the red pepper, scallions, celery, tomatoes, and hot pepper and cook, covered, until the vegetables are softened, about 5 minutes.

2. Add the crabmeat, evaporated skimmed milk, clam juice, and Old Bay Seasoning. Bring to a simmer and cook, stirring occasionally, for 3 minutes. Keep warm.

3. Meanwhile, in a large pot of boiling salted water, cook the pasta until just tender, 2 to 3 minutes. Drain and return to the pot.

(continued)

4. Add the crab mixture, toss well, and season to taste with salt (use a light touch—bottled clam juice can be salty). Transfer to a warmed serving bowl and serve immediately.

NUTRITIONAL ANALYSIS PER SERVING (BASED ON 8 SERVINGS)

CALORIES: 251 (30 percent from protein, 58 percent from carbohydrate, 11 percent from fat) • **PROTEIN:** 19 grams • **CARBOHYDRATE:** 36 grams • **FAT:** 3 grams • **CHOLESTEROL:** 55 milligrams • **SODIUM:** 287 milligrams

---

PASTA MYKONOS

MAKES 6 TO 8 SERVINGS

———

Practically every Greek taverna serves an oregano-scented tomato and shrimp dish dotted with feta cheese; I have paired it with a natural ally—pasta. The result is a dish with a thick and hearty sauce that clings to the pasta, perfect for supper after a rough day of lying around on Mediterranean shores. Unfortunately, low-fat feta cheese hasn't hit the dairy case yet, but many specialty grocers are carrying low-fat chèvre, which will provide the appropriate tang. If you can't find the chèvre, top each serving with a dollop of nonfat plain yogurt (which will save you a couple of fat grams).

———

2 teaspoons olive oil

3 scallions, chopped

2 garlic cloves, minced

2 pounds plum tomatoes, seeded and coarsely chopped

¼ cup white wine

2 tablespoons chopped fresh oregano or 2 teaspoons dried oregano

1 tablespoon chopped fresh mint or 1 teaspoon dried mint (optional)

½ teaspoon salt

¼ teaspoon crushed hot red pepper

12 ounces medium shrimp, peeled and deveined

12 ounces dried capellini (angel hair pasta)

12 Mediterranean black olives, pitted and coarsely chopped

4 ounces reduced-fat chèvre, crumbled, or feta cheese, well rinsed and crumbled

-----

1. In a large nonstick skillet, heat the oil over medium heat. Add the scallions and garlic and stir until the scallions are softened, about 1 minute. Add the tomatoes, wine, oregano, optional mint, salt, and hot red pepper, cover, and cook, stirring occasionally, until the tomatoes have given off their juices, about 5 minutes. Add the shrimp, cover, and cook just until the shrimp turn pink, 2 to 3 minutes. Keep warm.

2. Meanwhile, in a large pot of boiling salted water, cook the pasta until barely tender, 1 to 2 minutes; do not overcook. Drain well and return to the pot.

3. Add the sauce and olives to the pasta and toss well. Transfer to a warmed serving bowl, sprinkle with the cheese, and serve immediately.

NUTRITIONAL ANALYSIS PER SERVING (BASED ON 8 SERVINGS)

CALORIES: 306 (22 percent from protein, 53 percent from carbohydrate, 24 percent from fat) • **PROTEIN:** 17 grams • **CARBOHYDRATE:** 41 grams • **FAT:** 8 grams • **CHOLESTEROL:** 72 milligrams • **SODIUM:** 506 milligrams

SWORDFISH WITH SUN-DRIED TOMATO PESTO ON SHELLS

MAKES 6 TO 8 SERVINGS

Fresh swordfish, like salmon and tuna, is a pasta-friendly fish. Tossed with chunky sun-dried tomato and artichoke pesto and shell-shaped pasta, this dish is one I often serve to company. Using the pasta's cooking water to "loosen" the pesto for better distribution is a great trick—try it with any pesto, adding just enough of the water to make it noticeably thinner.

1½ pounds skinless swordfish steaks, cut into ¾-inch cubes
3 tablespoons fresh lemon juice
1 garlic clove, minced
Nonstick vegetable cooking spray
1 pound dried medium shell-shaped pasta
1 cup Sun-dried Tomato Pesto (189)
½ cup chopped fresh basil or ¼ cup chopped fresh parsley

1. In a medium bowl, sprinkle the swordfish cubes with the lemon juice and garlic. Spray a large nonstick skillet with nonstick cooking spray and heat over medium-high heat. Add the swordfish to the skillet and cook just until the fish is opaque, about 4 minutes; set aside.

2. In a large pot of boiling salted water, cook the pasta until just tender, about 9 minutes. Scoop out ¾ cup of the pasta cooking water and set aside; drain the pasta. Return the reserved pasta water to the pot, add the pesto, and mix well. Add the pasta and toss well.

3. Add the swordfish and basil to the pasta, toss well, and serve immediately.

NUTRIONAL ANALYSIS PER SERVING (BASED ON 8 SERVINGS)

CALORIES: 365 (30 percent from protein, 58 percent from carbohydrate, 13 percent from fat) • PROTEIN: 27 grams • CARBOHYDRATE: 52 grams • FAT: 5 grams • CHOLESTEROL: 35 milligrams • SODIUM: 173 milligrams

SHRIMP WITH TOMATOES AND CORN ON LINGUINE

MAKES 6 TO 8 SERVINGS

Here's an example of a colorful, tasty dish that is packed with protein, but not with fat. If you can't find cilantro, use another fresh herb such as dill or oregano, or even parsley.

Nonstick vegetable cooking spray
1 medium red onion, chopped
2 garlic cloves, minced
1 fresh hot chile pepper, such as jalapeño, seeded and minced
2½ pounds fresh plum tomatoes, seeded and chopped into
  ½-inch pieces
½ teaspoon salt
¼ teaspoon freshly ground black pepper
1 pound medium shrimp, peeled and deveined
1½ cups fresh or defrosted frozen corn kernels
1 pound freshly made or store-bought fresh cholesterol-free linguine
3 tablespoons chopped fresh cilantro

1. Lightly spray a large nonstick skillet with cooking spray and heat over medium heat. Add the onion, garlic, and hot pepper and cook, covered, until the onions have softened, about 3 minutes. Add the tomatoes, salt, and pepper and bring to a boil. Cover and cook until the tomatoes give off their juices, about 5 minutes.

2. Stir in the shrimp and corn. Cook, stirring occasionally, just until the shrimp are pink and firm, 2 to 3 minutes. Keep warm.

3. Meanwhile, in a large pot of boiling salted water, cook the pasta until just tender, 1 to 2 minutes. Drain well and return to the pot.

(continued)

4. Add the shrimp sauce and toss well. Transfer to a warmed serving bowl, sprinkle with the fresh cilantro, and serve immediately.

NUTRITIONAL ANALYSIS PER SERVING (BASED ON 8 SERVINGS)

CALORIES: 285 (25 percent from protein, 66 percent from carbohydrate, 9 percent from fat) • PROTEIN: 18 grams • CARBOHYDRATE: 48 grams • FAT: 3 grams • CHOLESTEROL: 87 milligrams • SODIUM: 282 milligrams

---

CLAMS IN TEQUILA-SPIKED TOMATO SAUCE ON VERMICELLI

MAKES 4 TO 6 SERVINGS

———

With chile pepper, garlic, and tequila, this tomato sauce really packs a punch, but the heady flavor is smoothed out by the creamy qualities of the evaporated skimmed milk and tempered with plenty of pasta.

———

36 small hard-shelled clams, such as littlenecks, well scrubbed and rinsed
1 28-ounce can whole tomatoes in juice, undrained
1 medium onion, coarsely chopped
1 fresh hot chile pepper, such as jalapeño, seeded and coarsely chopped
2 garlic cloves, crushed
2 teaspoons olive oil
½ cup evaporated skimmed milk
3 tablespoons tequila
12 ounces dried vermicelli
3 tablespoons chopped fresh cilantro

———

1. In a large bowl, soak the clams in lightly salted water while you prepare the other ingredients. (This helps rid the clams of grit. If you have the time, let them soak for 30 minutes. If the clams give off a lot of sand, and you're not too rushed, soak the clams for another 30 minutes in fresh lightly salted water.) Drain.

2. In a blender, process the tomatoes with their juice, the onion, hot pepper, and garlic until smooth.

3. In a large pot, heat the oil over high heat. Add the tomato puree with the evaporated skimmed milk, stir well, and cook until the liquid has evaporated by about half, 6 to 8 minutes. Stir in the tequila. Add the clams, cover, and cook until the clams open, about 5 minutes. Discard any clams that do not open. Keep warm.

4. Meanwhile, in a large pot of boiling salted water, cook the pasta until just tender, about 5 minutes. Drain.

5. Using tongs, transfer the pasta to individual deep soup bowls. Divide the clams among the bowls and ladle over the broth. Sprinkle each serving with cilantro, and serve immediately.

NUTRITIONAL ANALYSIS PER SERVING (BASED ON 6 SERVINGS)

CALORIES: 345 (19 percent from protein, 67 percent from carbohydrates, 9 percent from fat) • PROTEIN: 16 grams • CARBOHYDRATE: 58 grams • FAT: 3 grams • CHOLESTEROL: 15 milligrams • SODIUM: 290 milligrams

HERBED GARBANZOS AND PARSLEY WITH PENNE

MAKES 6 TO 8 SERVINGS

Be it ever so humble, this has become one of my favorite quick-to-fix suppers. It reminds me of hummus, only chewable. Be careful not to overcook the penne; it will be cooked further in the pasta pot with the lemon-scented broth.

2 teaspoons olive oil
1 medium red onion, chopped
2 garlic cloves, minced
1 16-ounce can garbanzo beans (chick-peas), drained and rinsed
1½ cups chicken stock, preferably homemade (page 212), or
　　low-sodium canned broth
Grated zest of 1 lemon
3 tablespoons fresh lemon juice
1 teaspoon ground cumin
¼ teaspoon dried oregano
¼ teaspoon salt
¼ teaspoon crushed hot red pepper
1 pound dried penne or other tubular pasta
1 cup chopped fresh parsley

1. In a large nonstick skillet, heat the oil over medium heat. Add the onion and garlic, cover, and cook until the onions are browned, about 5 minutes. Add the garbanzos, stock, lemon zest and juice, cumin, oregano, salt, and hot red pepper. Cover, reduce the heat to low, and simmer for 5 minutes.

2. Meanwhile, in a large pot of boiling salted water, cook the pasta until barely tender, about 7 minutes; do not overcook. Drain and return to the pot.

3. Add the garbanzo mixture and the parsley to the pasta, and cook over medium-low heat, stirring gently until the pasta has absorbed most of the liquid, 2 to 3 minutes. Transfer to a warmed serving bowl and serve immediately.

NUTRITIONAL ANALYSIS PER SERVING (BASED ON 8 SERVINGS)

CALORIES: 292 (14 percent from protein, 76 percent from carbohydrate, 10 percent from fat) • PROTEIN: 10 grams • CARBOHYDRATE: 55 grams • FAT: 3 grams • CHOLESTEROL: 0 milligrams • SODIUM: 345 milligrams

ARTICHOKE, TURKEY HAM, AND SUN-DRIED TOMATO FETTUCCINE

MAKES 6 TO 8 SERVINGS

———

I love sun-dried tomatoes, but you have to know what you're buying. Sometimes the Italian ones are overly salted, and many American brands are treated with sulphur dioxide to preserve them and keep them soft. Actually, a leathery sun-dried tomato is good, as that means that it has been naturally dehydrated, not salted, and is preservative-free. Make this dish using my quick microwave soaking method, but remember: It's only as good as your sun-dried tomatoes. Choose them with care.

———

2 ounces loose-packed sun-dried tomatoes
2 teaspoons olive oil
2 medium shallots, minced
1 garlic clove, minced
1 9-ounce package frozen artichoke hearts, defrosted and
   coarsely chopped
4 ounces turkey ham, cut into ½-inch cubes
¼ teaspoon salt
¼ teaspoon freshly ground black pepper
1 cup evaporated skimmed milk
¾ cup chicken stock, preferably homemade (page 212), or
   low-sodium canned broth
1 pound freshly made or store-bought fresh cholesterol-free fettuccine
2 tablespoons chopped fresh dill
6 tablespoons to ½ cup freshly grated imported Parmesan cheese

———

1. Place the sun-dried tomatoes in a small microwave-proof bowl and cover with hot water. Microwave the sun-dried tomatoes on high until softened, 3 to 6 minutes, depending on the dryness of the tomatoes. Drain, pat dry with paper towels, and cut into ¼-inch strips. Set aside.

2. In a medium nonstick skillet, heat the oil over medium heat. Add the shallots and garlic and stir until the shallots are softened, about 2 minutes. Add the artichoke hearts, turkey ham, salt, and pepper and cook, stirring, for 1 minute. Add the evaporated skimmed milk and stock and bring to a boil. Reduce the heat to low and simmer for 5 minutes.

3. Meanwhile, in a large pot of boiling salted water, cook the pasta until just tender, about 3 minutes. Drain well and return to the pot.

4. Add the artichoke mixture, the sun-dried tomatoes, and dill to the pasta and stir well. Transfer to a warmed serving bowl and serve immediately, sprinkling each serving with 1 tablespoon Parmesan cheese.

NUTRITIONAL ANALYSIS PER SERVING (BASED ON 8 SERVINGS)

CALORIES: 301 (22 percent from protein, 60 percent from carbohydrate, 19 percent from fat) • PROTEIN: 17 grams • CARBOHYDRATE: 45 grams • FAT: 6 grams • CHOLESTEROL: 16 milligrams • SODIUM: 503 milligrams

WHITE BEANS AND TOMATOES WITH SPAGHETTI

MAKES 6 SERVINGS

———

Individually, pasta and beans are bland, but combined and balanced with bright seasonings, they sing. Here, cubes of plum tomatoes and a good infusion of sage, garlic, and crushed red peppers work wonders. Freshly cooked white beans are best, so you can use the bean's thick, flavorful cooking liquid. The drained liquid from canned beans will work, but you may prefer to substitute homemade or low-sodium canned chicken broth.

———

2 teaspoons olive oil
1 large red onion, chopped
2 garlic cloves, minced
12 medium plum tomatoes (about 1½ pounds), seeded and chopped
1 cup reserved bean cooking liquid (see above), chicken broth, or
*   liquid from canned beans*
2 teaspoons chopped fresh sage or ¾ teaspoon crumbled dried sage
¼ teaspoon salt
¼ teaspoon crushed hot red pepper
2 cups cooked white beans (page 16)
1 pound dried spaghetti
¼ cup chopped fresh parsley

———

1. In a large nonstick skillet, heat the oil over medium heat. Add the onion and garlic and cook, covered, until the onion is softened, about 4 minutes. Add the tomatoes, reserved bean liquid, sage, salt, and crushed red pepper. Bring to a simmer, cover, and cook until the tomatoes are softened, about 5 minutes. Stir in the beans and cook until heated through, 2 to 3 minutes. Keep warm.

2. Meanwhile, in a large pot of boiling salted water, cook the spaghetti just until tender, about 7 minutes. Drain well and return to the pot.

3. Add the sauce and parsley to the pasta and toss well. Transfer to a warmed serving bowl, and serve immediately.

NUTRITIONAL ANALYSIS PER SERVING

CALORIES: 425 (15 percent from protein, 77 percent from carbohydrate, 8 percent from fat) • PROTEIN: 16 grams • CARBOHYDRATE: 82 grams • FAT: 4 grams • CHOLESTEROL: 0 milligrams • SODIUM: 108 milligrams

TURKEY, RED PEPPERS, AND SNAP PEAS WITH PENNE

MAKES 6 SERVINGS

Freshly roasted red peppers are always nice, but when the stopwatch is running in the kitchen, I often open a jar of the packed variety. (Be sure they are roasted red peppers, not the mildly flavored pimentos.) Teamed up with bright green sugar snap peas, they make a colorful pasta meal.

1 tablespoon olive oil
1 pound boneless, skinless turkey breast or turkey tenderloins,
   cut into strips 2 inches long and ½ inch thick
1 large red onion, halved lengthwise and sliced into half-moons
1 garlic clove, minced
¼ teaspoon salt
¼ teaspoon freshly ground black pepper
2 7-ounce jars roasted red peppers, rinsed, drained, and cut into
   ½-inch-wide strips
2 tablespoons all-purpose flour
1½ cups chicken stock, preferably homemade (page 212), or
   low-sodium canned broth
4 ounces sugar snap peas
1 pound dried penne or other tubular pasta

1. In a large nonstick skillet, heat the oil over medium-high heat. Add the turkey, onion, garlic, salt, and pepper and cook, stirring often, until the turkey is lightly browned and the onions are softened, about 5 minutes. Stir in the red pepper strips.

2. In a medium bowl, whisk the flour and ¼ cup of the chicken stock until smooth, then whisk in the remaining stock, and pour into the skillet. Bring to a simmer, reduce the heat to low, and cook, stirring often, until the turkey is cooked through, about 5 minutes. Keep warm.

3. Meanwhile, in a large pot of boiling salted water, cook the sugar snap peas until barely tender, about 1 minute. Using a large skimmer, remove the peas and stir into the sauce; set aside. Add the pasta to the boiling water and cook until just tender, about 8 minutes. Drain well and return to the pot.

4. Add the sauce and the reserved sugar snap peas to the pasta. Transfer to a warmed serving bowl, toss well, and serve immediately.

NUTRITIONAL ANALYSIS PER SERVING

CALORIES: 459 (26 percent from protein, 65 percent from carbohydrate, 9 percent from fat) • PROTEIN: 30 grams • CARBOHYDRATE: 73 grams • FAT: 5 grams • CHOLESTEROL: 47 milligrams • SODIUM: 886 milligrams

SCALLOPS IN ROSEMARY-VERMOUTH SAUCE ON LINGUINE

MAKES 6 SERVINGS

Scallops are one of my favorite ingredients when I'm cooking against the clock; they are at their best when quickly prepared. The complex herb flavor in dry vermouth is excellent here, but feel free to use a dry white wine if you prefer. If you can only find the larger sea scallops, simply cut them into three-quarter-inch cubes. (To remember the difference between the two kinds of scallops, just remind yourself that a bay is a smaller body of water than the sea—and therefore bay scallops are smaller than sea scallops.)

2 teaspoons olive oil
2 shallots, minced
1 garlic clove, minced
1 pound bay scallops, rinsed and patted dry
2 tablespoons all-purpose flour
¼ teaspoon freshly ground black pepper
1 cup bottled clam juice
¼ cup dry vermouth
1½ teaspoons chopped fresh rosemary or ½ teaspoon dried rosemary
½ cup evaporated skimmed milk
1 pound freshly made or store-bought fresh cholesterol-free linguine
3 plum tomatoes, seeded and cut into ¼-inch cubes
2 tablespoons chopped fresh parsley

1. In a large nonstick skillet, heat the oil over medium heat. Add the shallots and garlic and cook, stirring often, until the shallots are softened, about 1 minute.

2. In a medium bowl, toss the scallops with the flour and pepper. Add to the skillet, increase the heat to medium-high, and cook, stirring often, just until the scallops turn opaque, about 2 minutes. Transfer to a plate and set aside.

3. Add the clam juice, vermouth, and rosemary to the skillet and bring to a boil. Reduce the heat to low and simmer for 5 minutes. Return the scallops to the pan, add the evaporated milk, and bring just to a simmer; do not boil. Keep warm.

4. Meanwhile, in a large pot of boiling salted water, cook the pasta until just tender, about 2 minutes. Drain and return to the pot.

5. Add the scallop sauce, tomatoes, and parsley to the pasta. Toss well and serve immediately.

NUTRITIONAL ANALYSIS PER SERVING

CALORIES: 371 (26 percent from protein, 59 percent from carbohydrate, 12 percent from fat) • PROTEIN: 24 grams • CARBOHYDRATE: 54 grams • FAT: 5 grams • CHOLESTEROL: 26 milligrams • SODIUM: 383 milligrams

SAUTÉED SCALLOPS WITH CONFETTI VEGETABLES AND LINGUINE

MAKES 6 TO 8 SERVINGS

A "confetti" of finely chopped green zucchini and sweet red pepper makes this a colorful dish indeed. If you can only get the larger sea scallops, cut them into three-quarter-inch cubes. This dish is equally delicious when made with shrimp instead of scallops.

2 teaspoons olive oil
12 ounces small bay scallops, rinsed and patted dry
1 cup bottled clam juice
1 small zucchini, well scrubbed and cut into ¼-inch cubes
1 medium red bell pepper, stemmed, seeded, and cut into
    ¼-inch pieces
1 small white onion, finely chopped
1 garlic clove, minced
2 tablespoons fresh lemon juice
¼ teaspoon crushed hot red pepper
2 tablespoons finely chopped fresh basil
1 pound freshly made or store-bought fresh cholesterol-free linguine
Salt, to taste

1. In a large nonstick pan, heat the oil over medium-high heat. Add the scallops and cook, stirring occasionally, until opaque, about 2 minutes. Using a slotted spoon, transfer to a plate and set aside.

2. Add the clam juice, zucchini, bell pepper, onion, garlic, lemon juice, and hot red pepper to the skillet and bring to a simmer over medium-low heat. Cover and cook until the vegetables are softened, about 5 minutes. Return the scallops to the pan, add the basil, and cook, uncovered, for 1 minute. Keep warm.

3. Meanwhile, in a large pot of boiling salted water, cook the pasta until just tender, 1 to 2 minutes. Drain and return to the pot.

4. Add the scallop mixture, toss well, and season to taste with salt (use a light touch—bottled clam juice can be salty). Transfer to a warmed serving bowl and serve immediately.

NUTRITIONAL ANALYSIS PER SERVING (BASED ON 8 SERVINGS)
CALORIES: 239 (24 percent from protein, 63 percent from carbohydrate, 13 percent from fat) • PROTEIN: 14 grams • CARBOHYDRATE: 37 grams • FAT: 4 grams • CHOLESTEROL: 14 milligrams • SODIUM: 244 milligrams

VERMICELLI WITH SIZZLING ORANGE SHRIMP

MAKES 6 SERVINGS

This Chinese-inspired dish gets plenty of zip from plum sauce, orange zest, Szechuan peppercorns, and red pepper. The slightly sweet, slightly spicy sauce is a perfect foil for the shrimp.

Grated zest and juice of 1 large orange
2 tablespoons low-sodium soy sauce
1 teaspoon honey
1 garlic clove, finely chopped
¼ teaspoon crushed Szechuan peppercorns
½ teaspoon crushed hot red pepper
1 pound medium shrimp, shelled and deveined
1 cup chicken stock, preferably homemade (page 212), or
   low-sodium canned broth
¼ cup Chinese plum sauce, solids chopped
1 pound dried vermicelli
2 scallions, thinly sliced

(continued)

1. In a small bowl, combine the orange zest and juice, soy sauce, honey, garlic, Szechuan peppercorns, and hot red pepper. Add the shrimp and marinate for 10 to 20 minutes. Drain, reserving the marinade.

2. Spray a large nonstick skillet with vegetable cooking spray and heat over high heat. Add the shrimp and cook, turning often, just until the shrimp are firm and pink, about 2 minutes. Transfer to a plate and set aside.

3. Add the stock, plum sauce, and the reserved marinade to the skillet and bring to a boil over high heat. Cook until the liquid has reduced to about ¾ cup. Return the shrimp to the skillet and cook until heated through, about 1 minute. Keep warm.

4. Meanwhile, in a large pot of boiling salted water, cook the pasta until just tender, about 6 minutes. Drain well and return to the pot.

5. Add the shrimp sauce and scallions and toss well. Transfer to a warmed serving platter and serve immediately.

NUTRITIONAL ANALYSIS PER SERVING

CALORIES: 400 (24 percent from protein, 71 percent from carbohydrate, 5 percent from fat) • PROTEIN: 23 grams • CARBOHYDRATE: 70 grams • FAT: 2 grams • CHOLESTEROL: 116 milligrams • SODIUM: 505 milligrams

Garden Patch Pastas

❖❖❖

I'm very lucky to have access to beautiful produce. There's a year-round farmers' market nearby, and I have friends in the country who live surrounded by excellent produce stands.

Some of these recipes in this chapter rely on classic summer flavors—ripe plum tomatoes, green herbs fresh from the garden, tender summer squash—but these are not the only choices for a vegetable pasta. Rather than expect the anemic tomatoes that are the only ones I can get in February to produce a wonderful sauce, I either use excellent canned tomatoes or, better yet, make a pasta dish with the vegetables that are in season and full of flavor. In the cold months, I make pastas with mushrooms, cabbage, leeks, cauliflower, kale, and other winter vegetables. In the spring, I could eat asparagus and sugar snap peas every day, and I am always looking for ways to use them.

Vegetable stock is used to marry the flavors and act as a sauce in many of these dishes. There is a recipe for rich, garlic-scented homemade vegetable stock on page 220. If you are not vegetarian, you can use chicken stock instead of vegetable, but again, homemade is preferred (page 212). Canned vegetable and chicken broths are available (the versions at natural food stores are the best), but homemade stocks take just a little time to put together, and hardly any effort.

PASTA WITH SALSA CRUDA

MAKES 6 TO 8 SERVINGS

Here is one of the simplest, but most delicious meals one could possibly serve on a hot summer's evening. Only the pasta itself needs to be cooked and the dish is even tasty served lukewarm. Choose the plumpest, ripest plum tomatoes and most fragrant fresh basil you can find. Don't even think of making this with musty dried basil and innocuous supermarket tomatoes!

SALSA CRUDA

7 *ripe medium plum tomatoes (about 2 pounds), cored and cut into* ½-inch cubes
½ *cup chopped fresh basil*
2 *garlic cloves, crushed through a press*
1 *tablespoon extra-virgin olive oil*
1 *tablespoon red wine vinegar*
½ *teaspoon salt, or more to taste*
¼ *teaspoon freshly ground black pepper, or more to taste*

1 *pound dried spaghetti*

---

1. Make the Salsa: In a large bowl, combine all of the ingredients. Cover with plastic wrap and let stand at room temperature for at least 2 hours, or up to 6 hours.

2. When ready to serve, in a large pot of boiling salted water, cook the pasta until just tender, about 7 minutes. Drain well and transfer to a warmed serving bowl.

3. Add the tomato mixture and toss well, seasoning to taste with additional salt and pepper if necessary. Serve immediately.

Note: Plum tomatoes work best here, as beefsteaks have a tendency to give off too much juice. If you are using large tomatoes, cut them in half through their "equator," and squeeze them gently to remove excess seeds and juice. A combination of red and yellow tomatoes makes a spectacular-looking salsa. I often use a combination of fresh herbs in tandem with the basil (oregano and marjoram being my favorites).

NUTRITIONAL ANALYSIS PER SERVING (BASED ON 8 SERVINGS)

CALORIES: 266 (13 percent from protein, 76 percent from carbohydrate, 11 percent from fat) • PROTEIN: 9 grams • CARBOHYDRATE: 51 grams • FAT: 3 grams • CHOLESTEROL: 0 milligrams • SODIUM: 145 milligrams

---

ROTINI WITH NORMA'S
EGGPLANT SAUCE

MAKES 6 TO 8 SERVINGS

This spicy sauce is one of the hallmarks of Sicilian cooking, named after the heroine of a favorite son's (Vincenzo Bellini) opera. Norma must have been a hearty eater, as this is an especially rich, though meatless, dish. Unless your eggplant is farmstand-fresh, I recommend salting it to minimize any bitter taste; if you are sure of its pedigree, you can skip this step. Be certain your oil is really hot before adding the eggplant so it begins to cook instantly and doesn't soak up too much oil.

1 medium eggplant (1 pound), trimmed and cut into 1-inch cubes
1 teaspoon salt
Nonstick vegetable cooking spray
1 large onion, chopped
2 garlic cloves, minced
1 tablespoon olive oil
1 28-ounce can whole tomatoes in juice, undrained, coarsely chopped
1½ teaspoons dried basil
1½ teaspoons dried oregano
½ teaspoon crushed hot red pepper
1 pound dried rotini or other spiral-shaped pasta
8 ounces nonfat ricotta cheese

1. In a colander, toss the eggplant with the salt. Set over a plate and let stand at least 30 minutes. Rinse well under cold running water, drain, and pat completely dry with paper towels.

2. Spray a large nonstick skillet with nonstick vegetable spray, and heat over medium heat. Add the onion and garlic, cover, and cook until the onion is softened, about 3 minutes. Transfer to a plate and set aside.

3. Add the oil to the skillet, and heat over medium-high heat until very hot but not smoking. (A piece of eggplant should sizzle immediately when put into the pan.) Add the eggplant and cook, turning occasionally, until lightly browned, about 5 minutes. Return the onion and garlic to the pan, add the tomatoes with their juices, the basil, oregano, and crushed red pepper, and bring to a simmer. Reduce the heat to low, cover, and simmer until the eggplant is tender, about 20 minutes. Uncover and cook, stirring often, until the sauce has thickened slightly, about 10 minutes. Keep warm.

4. Meanwhile, in a large pot of boiling salted water, cook the pasta until just tender, about 8 minutes. Drain and return to the pot.

5. Add the eggplant sauce and ricotta cheese to the pasta and toss well. Transfer to a warmed serving bowl and serve immediately.

NUTRITIONAL ANALYSIS PER SERVING (BASED ON 8 SERVINGS)

CALORIES: 313 (17 percent from protein, 74 percent from carbohydrate, 9 percent from fat) • PROTEIN: 14 grams • CARBOHYDRATE: 58 grams • FAT: 3 grams • CHOLESTEROL: 5 milligrams • SODIUM: 222 milligrams

SPAGHETTI PEPERONATA

MAKES 6 TO 8 SERVINGS

One of the most familiar sights on the antipasto table of an Italian trattoria is a large platter of *peperonata,* vibrantly colored roasted pepper strips in a tangy vinaigrette. In addition to its talents as an appetizer, peperonata makes an excellent pasta topping.

1 *tablespoon olive oil*
2 *medium onions, halved lengthwise and cut into* ¼*-inch-thick half-moons*
2 *garlic cloves, minced*
3 *large red bell peppers (or a combination of red and yellow peppers), stemmed, seeded, and cut into* ¼*-inch-wide strips*
3 *medium Italian frying peppers or 2 large green bell peppers, stemmed, seeded, and cut into* ¼*-inch-wide strips*
1 *teaspoon dried oregano*
¼ *teaspoon salt*
¼ *teaspoon crushed hot red pepper*
1 *tablespoon red wine vinegar*
¼ *teaspoon sugar*
1 *pound dried spaghetti*

1. In large nonstick skillet, heat the oil over medium heat. Add the onions and garlic, cover, and cook, stirring occasionally, until the onions are golden, about 4 minutes.

2. Add the pepper strips, oregano, salt, and crushed red pepper. Reduce the heat to medium-low, cover, and cook, stirring occasionally, until peppers are very soft, 20 to 30 minutes. Stir in the vinegar and sugar. Keep warm.

3. Meanwhile, in a large pot of boiling salted water, cook the pasta until just tender, about 7 minutes. Drain and return to the pot.

4. Add the peperonata and toss well. Transfer to a warmed serving dish and serve immediately.

NUTRITIONAL ANALYSIS PER SERVING (BASED ON 8 SERVINGS)

CALORIES: 277 (13 percent from protein, 78 percent from carbohydrate, 10 percent from fat) • PROTEIN: 9 grams • CARBOHYDRATE: 54 grams • FAT: 3 grams • CHOLESTEROL: 0 milligrams • SODIUM: 72 milligrams

PEPERONATA PASTA FRITTATA

MAKES 4 TO 6 SERVINGS

Creating a plump frittata is a tasty way to use leftover pasta. When visiting friends in the country, I often cook up extra pasta for Saturday night's supper—so we have leftovers to make a frittata for Sunday's lunch. My favorite frittata is made with leftover Spaghetti Peperonata, but tomato-sauced pastas are fine, too. It's great served with a spoonful of Salsa Cruda (page 166).

Nonstick vegetable cooking spray
3 cups leftover Spaghetti Peperonata (page 170)
1 cup liquid egg substitute
¼ teaspoon salt
⅛ teaspoon freshly ground black pepper

1. In a large bowl, combine the leftover pasta, liquid egg substitute, salt, and pepper; mix well.

2. Spray a medium nonstick skillet with cooking spray and heat over medium-high heat. Pour the frittata mixture into the skillet and spread to an even thickness. Cook until the underside is lightly browned (lift up an edge with a rubber spatula to check), about 3 minutes. Invert a flat plate over the skillet. Firmly holding the skillet and the plate together, invert the pan to turn the frittata out onto the plate. Return the skillet to the heat. Carefully slide the frittata back into the skillet, and continue cooking until the other side is lightly browned, 2 to 3 minutes.

3. Slide the frittata onto a serving platter, and serve hot, warm, or at room temperature, cut into wedges.

NUTRITIONAL ANALYSIS PER SERVING (BASED ON 6 SERVINGS)

CALORIES: 100 (29 percent from protein, 52 percent from carbohydrate, 19 percent from fat) • PROTEIN: 7 grams • CARBOHYDRATE: 13 grams • FAT: 2 grams • CHOLESTEROL: less than 1 milligram • SODIUM: 180 milligram

PASTA WITH MUSHROOM MARSALA

MAKES 6 TO 8 SERVINGS

Mushrooms and Marsala are a terrific team, and make a sensational pasta sauce. It is very important to use dry Marsala, not sweet. Dry Marsala is always used in savory dishes; the sweet is only appropriate in Italian desserts, such as pastries and zabaglione.

2 teaspoons olive oil
1 large onion, coarsely chopped
1 pound fresh mushrooms (white button, cremini, or portobello,
  or a combination), thinly sliced
½ cup dry Marsala
1 cup nonfat ricotta cheese
½ cup skim milk
¼ teaspoon salt
¼ teaspoon freshly ground black pepper
⅛ teaspoon freshly grated nutmeg
1 pound freshly made or store-bought fresh cholesterol-free
  fettuccine

1. In a large nonstick skillet, heat the oil over medium-high heat. Add the onion, cover, and cook, stirring occasionally, until the onions are golden, about 4 minutes. Add the mushrooms and Marsala. Cook, uncovered, stirring often, until all mushroom juices have evaporated and the mushrooms have begun to brown, about 7 minutes.

2. Meanwhile, in a blender or a food processor fitted with the metal blade, process the ricotta, skim milk, salt, pepper, and nutmeg until smooth.

3. Stir the ricotta mixture into the mushrooms, reduce the heat to low, and stir until the sauce is warmed through. Do not boil.

4. While the sauce is cooking, in a large pot of boiling salted water, cook the pasta until just tender, 2 to 3 minutes. Drain and return to the pot.

(continued)

5. Add the mushroom sauce and toss well. Transfer to a warmed serving bowl and serve immediately.

NUTRITIONAL ANALYSIS PER SERVING (BASED ON 8 SERVINGS)

CALORIES: 314 (18 percent from protein, 70 percent from carbohydrate, 7 percent from fat) • PROTEIN: 14 grams • CARBOHYDRATE: 55 grams • FAT: 3 grams • CHOLESTEROL: 5 milligrams • SODIUM: 140 milligrams

---

ZITI WITH MOROCCAN-SPICED BAKED EGGPLANT SAUCE

MAKES 6 TO 8 SERVINGS

This full-flavored sauce was inspired by a Moroccan tomato and eggplant "salad" described by Paula Wolfert in her *World of Food* (HarperCollins, 1990). Rather than deep-frying eggplant slices the Moroccan way, I roast the eggplants until they are so tender they collapse, then simmer the pulp with tomatoes and spices.

---

2 small eggplants (about 12 ounces each)
1 tablespoon olive oil
1 medium onion, chopped
2 garlic cloves, minced
1 28-ounce can crushed tomatoes
1½ teaspoons sweet Hungarian paprika
1 teaspoon ground cumin
¼ teaspoon salt
⅛ teaspoon cayenne pepper
2 tablespoons fresh lemon juice
1 pound dried ziti or other tubular pasta

• MR. PASTA'S HEALTHY PASTA COOKBOOK •

1. Preheat the oven to 400°F.

2. Brush the eggplants lightly with about 1 teaspoon of the oil. Place on a baking sheet and roast until very soft and collapsed, about 45 minutes. Cool completely.

3. Using a serrated knife, cut the cooled eggplants in half lengthwise. Scoop out the softened flesh with a large spoon, and discard the skin.

4. In a large nonstick skillet, heat the remaining oil over medium heat. Add the onion and garlic, cover, and cook until the onions are golden, about 4 minutes. Stir in the eggplant flesh, tomatoes, paprika, cumin, salt, and cayenne pepper, and bring to a simmer. Reduce the heat to low and cook, partially covered, until the sauce has thickened slightly, about 25 minutes. Remove from the heat, and stir in the lemon juice.

5. Meanwhile, in a large pot of boiling salted water, cook the pasta until just tender, about 8 minutes. Drain and return to the pot.

6. Add the eggplant sauce to the pasta and mix well. Transfer to a warm serving bowl and serve immediately.

NUTRITIONAL ANALYSIS PER SERVING (BASED ON 8 SERVINGS)

CALORIES: 284 (13 percent from protein, 77 percent from carbohydrate, 10 percent from fat) • PROTEIN: 9 grams • CARBOHYDRATE: 55 grams • FAT: 3 grams • CHOLESTEROL: 0 milligrams • SODIUM: 233 milligrams

---

VEGETARIAN LASAGNE

Good lasagne is never quick to make, but your efforts will be rewarded when you serve this mouth-watering version, with its mélange of roasted zucchini, eggplant, and red bell peppers. The problem with many vegetable lasagne is that they can be watery, but here the excess moisture is removed by the salting and roasting procedures.

Nonstick vegetable cooking spray
2 large zucchini, well scrubbed, trimmed, halved crosswise, and cut
*   lengthwise into ¼-inch-thick slices*
2 medium eggplants (about 1 pound each), trimmed and cut into
*   ½-inch-thick rounds*
1 tablespoon salt
3 large red bell peppers
12 dried lasagne noodles (9 ounces)
4 cups Herbed Marinara Sauce (page 90)
1 cup nonfat ricotta cheese
1 cup shredded nonfat mozzarella cheese (4 ounces)

---

1. Preheat the oven to 450°F. Lightly spray two large baking sheets and a 13- by 9-inch baking dish with nonstick cooking spray.

2. Place the zucchini and eggplant in two separate large bowls. Sprinkle each vegetable with 1½ teaspoons of the salt, toss well, and let stand at least 30 minutes. Then rinse well with cold water to remove the salt, drain, and pat completely dry with paper towels.

3. Meanwhile, place the bell peppers on a baking sheet and roast, turning occasionally, until the skins are charred and blistered, about 30 minutes. Transfer to a bag, close, and let stand 20 minutes. Remove and discard the stems, skin, and seeds. Cut the roasted peppers into 2-inch-wide strips and set aside on paper towels to drain.

4. Place the drained zucchini and eggplant on separate baking sheets. Roast until just crisp-tender, about 15 minutes. Do not overbake the vegetables; they should hold their shape. Pat the zucchini dry with paper towels. Reduce the oven temperature to 375°F.

5. While the zucchini and eggplant are roasting, cook the lasagne noodles in a large pot of boiling salted water, until barely tender, about 9 minutes. (Do not overcook; the pasta will cook further during baking.) Drain, and rinse under cold water. To keep the noodles from sticking together, place them in a bowl with cold water to cover.

6. Spread a thin layer of the tomato sauce over the bottom of the prepared baking dish. Remove 4 noodles from the water and drain well. Arrange them, slightly overlapping, in the baking dish. Layer the eggplant over the noodles, and top with half of the red pepper strips. Spoon half of the ricotta over the vegetables, and sprinkle with half of the mozzarella. Spread one third of the remaining tomato sauce over the cheese. Arrange another layer of drained noodles over the sauce. Layer the zucchini over the noodles, then top with the remaining pepper strips, ricotta, and mozzarella. Spread with half of the remaining sauce, and arrange a final layer of drained noodles, over the sauce. Top with the remaining sauce. Cover with aluminum foil. (The lasagne can be prepared up to 6 hours ahead, covered, and refrigerated. Remove from the refrigerator 30 minutes before baking.)

7. Bake the lasagne for 20 minutes. Remove the foil and bake until bubbling and heated through, about 20 minutes. Let stand about 10 minutes before cutting into rectangles to serve.

NUTRITIONAL ANALYSIS PER SERVING (BASED ON 12 SERVINGS)

CALORIES: 176 (23 percent from protein, 69 percent from carbohydrate, 8 percent from fat) • PROTEIN: 11 grams • CARBOHYDRATE: 32 grams • FAT: 2 grams • CHOLESTEROL: 5 milligrams • SODIUM: 245 milligrams

LINGUINE WITH CHUNKY ROASTED PEPPER CREAM

MAKES 4 TO 6 SERVINGS

It's so simple to roast garlic and peppers, and the trip to the oven mellows their flavors nicely.

---

1 *head garlic, with nice plump cloves*
6 *medium red bell peppers*
¾ *cup nonfat ricotta cheese*
⅓ *cup skim milk*
¼ *teaspoon salt*
⅛ *teaspoon cayenne pepper*
1 *pound freshly made or store-bought fresh cholesterol-free linguine*
2 *tablespoons chopped fresh basil*

---

1. Preheat the oven to 450°F.

2. Loosely wrap the head of garlic in aluminum foil. Place the bell peppers and garlic on a baking sheet and place in the oven. Roast the garlic until it is soft when squeezed (protect your hands with a kitchen towel), about 20 minutes. Remove the garlic from the oven and set aside. Continue roasting the bell peppers, turning occasionally, until the skins are charred and blistered, about 15 more minutes. Transfer to a bag, close, and let stand 20 minutes.

3. Remove and discard the stems, skin, and seeds from the roasted peppers. Cut half of the peppers into ¾-inch strips and set the strips aside. Place the remaining peppers in a blender. Cut the garlic in half horizontally, squeeze out the softened pulp, and add the pulp to the blender. Add the ricotta cheese, skim milk, salt, and cayenne pepper, and process until smooth.

4. Meanwhile, in a large pot of boiling salted water, cook the pasta until just tender, 2 to 3 minutes. Drain briefly, letting some water cling to the pasta; return to the pot.

5. Add the red pepper sauce, red pepper strips, and basil to the pasta and toss well. Transfer to a warm serving dish, and serve immediately.

NUTRITIONAL ANALYSIS PER SERVING (BASED ON 6 SERVINGS)

CALORIES: 290 (19 percent from protein, 72 percent from carbohydrate, 9 percent from fat) • PROTEIN: 14 grams • CARBOHYDRATE: 52 grams • FAT: 3 grams • CHOLESTEROL: 5 milligrams • SODIUM: 181 milligrams

ZUCCHINI COINS WITH BUCATINI

MAKES 6 TO 8 SERVINGS

———

The trick to this pasta is to get the zucchini rounds nicely browned without scorching them. As salt will draw out the zucchini's moisture, and moisture inhibits browning, don't season the zucchini until it's well browned. While I make this dish year-round, it's particularly delicious in the summer when the zucchini is just a bit too abundant and the mint is running rampant in the garden.

———

1 tablespoon olive oil
2 medium zucchini (about 1 pound), well scrubbed, trimmed, and
    cut into ⅛-inch-thick rounds
1 garlic clove, crushed through a press
¼ teaspoon salt
¼ teaspoon freshly ground black pepper
1 pound dried bucatini (hollow spaghetti) or linguine
½ cup chicken stock, preferably homemade (page 212), or
    low-sodium canned broth
2 tablespoons fresh lemon juice
1 tablespoon chopped fresh mint or 1 teaspoon dried mint
6 tablespoons to ½ cup freshly grated imported Parmesan cheese

———

1. In a large nonstick skillet, heat the oil over medium-high heat until very hot but not smoking. Cook the zucchini, turning occasionally, until golden brown, 6 to 8 minutes. During the last minute of cooking, add in the garlic, salt, and pepper.

2. Meanwhile, in a large pot of boiling salted water, cook the pasta until just tender, about 8 minutes. Drain well and return to the pot.

3. While the pasta is cooking, in a small saucepan, bring the chicken broth and the lemon juice to a simmer over low heat. Keep warm.

4. Add the zucchini, warm broth, and mint to the pasta and toss well. Serve immediately, sprinkling each serving with 1 tablespoon Parmesan cheese.

Note: If fresh mint leaves are not available, substitute 2 tablespoons finely chopped fresh parsley combined with ½ teaspoon dried mint leaves.

NUTRITIONAL ANALYSIS PER SERVING (BASED ON 8 SERVINGS)

CALORIES: 279 (15 percent from protein, 69 percent from carbohydrate, 15 percent from fat) • PROTEIN: 11 grams • CARBOHYDRATE: 48 grams • FAT: 5 grams • CHOLESTEROL: 5 milligrams • SODIUM: 229 milligrams

MOSTACCIOLI WITH CAULIFLOWER AND SPICY CRUMBS

MAKES 6 TO 8 SERVINGS

Here's a great wintertime pasta entrée. I actually look forward to having stale pieces of Italian bread so I can turn them into the crisp crumbs required for this dish. Sandy dried bread crumbs from a box just won't do.

1 large head cauliflower (about 2 pounds), trimmed and cut into
florets
1 pound dried mostaccioli or other tubular pasta
8 anchovy fillets packed in olive oil, drained (reserve 2 teaspoons of
the anchovy oil), rinsed, and finely chopped to a paste
2 garlic cloves, minced
1 cup freshly made dried bread crumbs (see page 17)
½ teaspoon crushed hot red pepper

1. In a large pot of boiling salted water, cook the cauliflower until tender, 5 to 7 minutes. Using a wire sieve, scoop out the cauliflower and transfer to a colander. Rinse under cold water and set aside.

2. Add the pasta to the pot of boiling water and cook until just tender, about 8 minutes. During the last minute, add the reserved cauliflower to the water to reheat. Drain the pasta and cauliflower.

3. Meanwhile, in a medium nonstick skillet, combine the chopped anchovies, the reserved 2 teaspoons anchovy oil, and the garlic and cook over medium heat, stirring often, until the garlic is golden, about 1 minute. Add the bread crumbs and crushed red pepper and cook, stirring often, until the crumbs are toasted, about 3 minutes. Transfer to a plate and set aside.

4. Transfer the pasta and cauliflower to a warmed serving bowl, and sprinkle with the crumb mixture. Toss just before serving.

NUTRITIONAL ANALYSIS PER SERVING (BASED ON 8 SERVINGS)

CALORIES: 321 (16 percent from protein, 75 percent from carbohydrate, 10 percent from fat) • PROTEIN: 13 grams • CARBOHYDRATE: 60 grams • FAT: 3 grams • CHOLESTEROL: 3 milligrams • SODIUM: 259 milligrams

PENNE WITH SMOTHERED SWISS CHARD AND LEEKS

MAKES 6 TO 8 SERVINGS

Red wine adds a touch of acidity that I like with chard and leeks. Be sure to rinse these vegetables well—grit hides easily in their nooks and crannies, and one speck of sand can ruin the whole dish!

1 bunch Swiss chard (about 1¾ pounds)
1 cup chicken stock, preferably homemade (page 212), or
   low-sodium canned broth
4 medium leeks, trimmed, chopped, and well rinsed
½ cup dry red wine
2 teaspoons chopped fresh rosemary or ½ teaspoon dried rosemary
¼ teaspoon salt
¼ teaspoon freshly ground black pepper
1 pound dried penne or other tubular pasta
½ cup nonfat ricotta cheese, at room temperature

(continued)

1. Separate the chard leaves from the stems and coarsely chop the stems. Stack the leaves, slice them lengthwise in half, and then cut crosswise into 1-inch-wide strips. Drop into a sink filled with cool water and agitate briskly with your hands. Lift the leaves and stems from the water, leaving any dirt and grit in the bottom of the sink, and transfer to a bowl. Set aside.

2. In a large nonstick skillet over medium-low heat, combine the stock, leeks, and wine and bring to a simmer. Cover and cook until the leeks are very soft, about 15 minutes. Increase the heat to medium-high, and add the chard in batches, covering the pan and waiting for each batch to wilt before adding the next one. Stir in the rosemary, salt, and pepper. Reduce the heat to medium-low, cover, and cook until the chard is tender, 10 to 15 minutes.

3. Meanwhile, in a large pot of boiling salted water, cook the pasta until just tender, about 8 minutes. Drain and return to the pot.

4. Stir the chard mixture and ricotta cheese into the pasta. Transfer to a warmed serving bowl and serve immediately.

NUTRITIONAL ANALYSIS PER SERVING (BASED ON 8 SERVINGS)
CALORIES: 307 (16 percent from protein, 76 percent from carbohydrate, 4 percent from fat) • **PROTEIN:** 13 grams • **CARBOHYDRATE:** 59 grams • **FAT:** 1 gram • **CHOLESTEROL:** 2 milligrams • **SODIUM:** 373 milligrams

---

FETTUCCINE WITH ARUGULA PESTO

MAKES 6 TO 8 SERVINGS

———

Arugula can be delicious, but, in my opinion, it is a little too strongly flavored to stand on its own as a flavoring agent. This pesto tempers its peppery taste with ricotta; the pesto is then tossed with plum tomato chunks to make a delicious and very easy pasta sauce.

———

Arugula Pesto

1 bunch arugula, stems removed and well rinsed (about 2 packed
cups leaves)
1 garlic clove, minced
1 cup nonfat ricotta cheese
¼ teaspoon salt
¼ teaspoon freshly ground black pepper

1 pound freshly made or store-bought fresh cholesterol-free
fettuccine
6 large ripe plum tomatoes (about 1 pound), seeded and cut into
½-inch pieces
4-ounces imported Parmesan cheese in one chunk

———

1. Make the arugula pesto: In a food processor fitted with the metal blade, process the arugula, garlic, ricotta, salt, and pepper until smooth, scraping down the sides of the bowl as needed. (The pesto can be prepared up to 2 days ahead, tightly covered, and refrigerated. Bring to room temperature before serving.)

2. In a large pot of boiling salted water, cook the pasta until just tender, 2 to 3 minutes. Scoop out ⅓ cup of the pasta cooking water and set aside. Drain the pasta.

3. Add the pesto and reserved pasta water to the empty pot and mix well to "loosen" the pesto. Add the pasta and tomatoes and toss well. Transfer to a warmed serving bowl.

4. Using a swivel-bladed vegetable peeler, press firmly to shave "curls" from the chunk of Parmesan over the pasta. You will need only about 1 ounce of the cheese. Save the remaining cheese for another use. Bring to the table, then toss again and serve immediately.

NUTRITIONAL ANALYSIS PER SERVING (BASED ON 8 SERVINGS)

CALORIES: 224 (22 percent from protein, 65 percent from carbohydrate, 13 percent from fat) • PROTEIN: 12 grams • CARBOHYDRATE: 37 grams • FAT: 3 grams • CHOLESTEROL: 7 milligrams • SODIUM: 211 milligrams

FETTUCCINE WITH SAUTÉED RADICCHIO AND CARAMELIZED ONIONS

MAKES 6 TO 8 SERVINGS

Most cooks are familiar with radicchio as a salad vegetable, but it is equally fine when cooked. Its mildly bitter flavor is complemented by the sweetness of long-cooked red onions. My guests are intrigued and pleased by this combination—as appropriate as the first course for an elegant dinner as for the main course of family supper.

-----

1 tablespoon olive oil
2 large red onions, thinly sliced
¼ cup chicken stock, preferably homemade (page 212), or
   low-sodium canned broth
½ teaspoon sugar
2 ounces thinly sliced prosciutto, trimmed of visible fat and
   coarsely chopped
1 garlic clove, minced
2 medium heads or 1 large head radicchio (about 12 ounces), cored,
   quartered, and cut into 2-inch pieces
½ cup evaporated skimmed milk
Salt, to taste
¼ teaspoon freshly ground black pepper
1 pound freshly made or store-bought fresh cholesterol-free
   fettuccine

-----

1. In a large nonstick skillet, heat the oil over medium heat. Add the onions, cover, and cook, stirring occasionally, until the onions are very soft and golden, about 8 minutes. Add the sugar and continue to cook, stirring often, until the onions are caramelized and deeply browned, about 10 minutes.

2. Add the prosciutto and garlic and stir for 1 minute. Add the radicchio in two batches, covering the skillet and letting the first batch wilt slightly before adding the next. Then cook, covered, until the radicchio is soft, about 10 minutes. Stir in the evaporated milk, salt and pepper (the amount of salt needed depends on the saltiness of the prosciutto). Keep warm.

3. Meanwhile, in a large pot of boiling salted water, cook the pasta until just tender, 2 to 3 minutes. Drain and return to the pot.

4. Add the sauce and toss well. Transfer to a warmed serving bowl and serve immediately.

NUTRITIONAL ANALYSIS PER SERVING (BASED ON 8 SERVINGS)

CALORIES: 272 (17 percent from protein, 61 percent from carbohydrate, 22 percent from fat) • PROTEIN: 12 grams • CARBOHYDRATE: 42 grams • FAT: 7 grams • CHOLESTEROL: less than 1 milligram • SODIUM: 250 milligrams

---

LINGUINE WITH BROCCOLI PESTO

MAKES 6 TO 8 SERVINGS

Who says pesto has to be made from herbs? If you use a bulky vegetable, like broccoli, you can get the thickness of pesto without all the oil. This has made numerous command repeat performances at my dinner table.

2 garlic cloves, crushed

1 teaspoon extra-virgin olive oil

3 cups broccoli florets (about 9 ounces), from 1 large bunch

1 cup chicken stock, preferably homemade (page 212), or low-sodium canned broth

¼ teaspoon salt

¼ teaspoon crushed hot red pepper

¼ cup chopped fresh basil or 2 teaspoons dried basil

1 pound dried linguine

4 ripe plum tomatoes, seeded and chopped

6 tablespoons to ½ cup freshly grated imported Parmesan cheese

1. In a large nonstick skillet, cook the garlic in the oil over medium heat, stirring often, until the garlic is barely golden, about 2 minutes. Add the broccoli, chicken stock, salt, and crushed red pepper and bring to a simmer. Cover, reduce the heat to medium-low, and simmer until the broccoli is very tender, about 10 minutes. Transfer to a blender or a food processor fitted with the metal blade, add the basil, and process until smooth.

2. Meanwhile, in a large pot of boiling salted water, cook the pasta until just tender, about 8 minutes. Drain, and return to the pot.

3. Pour the broccoli pesto over the pasta and toss well. Sprinkle with the chopped tomatoes. Serve immediately, topping each serving with 1 tablespoon Parmesan cheese.

NUTRITIONAL ANALYSIS PER SERVING (BASED ON 8 SERVINGS)

CALORIES: 285 (17 percent from protein, 71 percent from carbohydrate, 12 percent from fat) • PROTEIN: 12 grams • CARBOHYDRATE: 51 grams • FAT: 4 grams • CHOLESTEROL: 5 milligrams • SODIUM: 286 milligrams

SPAGHETTI WITH SUN-DRIED TOMATO PESTO

MAKES 6 TO 8 SERVINGS

Sun-dried tomatoes are bursting with flavor—no wonder they've become a staple in the new American kitchen. (See my shopping tips for sun-dried tomatoes on page 23.) This pesto combines them with equally flavorful Mediterranean olives and herbs for a pasta sauce that is as delicious as it is brassy.

SUN-DRIED TOMATO PESTO

4 ounces loose-packed sun-dried tomatoes
¼ cup coarsely chopped pitted, Mediterranean black olives
1 garlic clove, minced
1 teaspoon fresh rosemary or ½ teaspoon dried rosemary
1 teaspoon fresh thyme leaves or ½ teaspoon dried thyme
¼ teaspoon crushed hot red pepper
1 cup chicken stock, preferably homemade (page 212), or
   low-sodium canned broth

1 pound dried spaghetti

---

1. Make the pesto: In a medium bowl, cover the sun-dried tomatoes with boiling water. Let stand until softened, from 3 to 30 minutes, depending on the dryness of the tomatoes. Drain well, and transfer to a food processor fitted with the metal blade or a blender.

2. Add the olives, garlic, rosemary, thyme, and hot red pepper and process until chopped. With the machine running, gradually add the chicken stock, scraping down the sides of the container as needed, and process until smooth. (The pesto can be prepared up to 2 days ahead, tightly covered, and refrigerated. Bring to room temperature before serving.)

3. Meanwhile, in a large pot of boiling salted water, cook the pasta until just tender, about 7 minutes. Scoop out ½ cup of the pasta cooking water and set aside. Drain the pasta and return to the pot.

(continued)

4. Add the pesto and reserved cooking water to the pasta and toss well. Transfer to a warmed serving bowl and serve immediately.

NUTRITIONAL ANALYSIS PER SERVING (BASED ON 8 SERVINGS)

CALORIES: 280 (14 percent from protein, 78 percent from carbohydrate, 8 percent from fat) • PROTEIN: 10 grams • CARBOHYDRATE: 56 grams • FAT: 3 grams • CHOLESTEROL: 0 milligrams • SODIUM: 222 milligrams

---

SPRINGTIME SUGAR SNAP AND HERB PASTA

MAKES 6 TO 8 SERVINGS

This refreshing dish was inspired by a mound of emerald-green sugar snap peas I purchased at the farmers' market one bright spring morning. Although a good cook always aspires to use the best ingredients, it's imperative in such a simple dish as this. Use only crisp peas, a full-flavored vegetable broth, fragrant herbs, and fresh-as-can-be pasta. If you make your own pasta, try Golden Carrot Pasta (page 42).

1½ cups vegetable broth, preferably homemade (page 220)
1 pound sugar snap peas, rinsed and trimmed
1 pound freshly made or store-bought fresh cholesterol-free
  fettuccine
2 tablespoons chopped fresh chives, mint, or tarragon
¼ teaspoon freshly ground black pepper, or more to taste

---

1. In a large skillet over high heat, bring the vegetable stock to a boil. Add the sugar snap peas and cook until they are bright green, but still crisp, about 1 minute.

2. Meanwhile, in a large pot of boiling salted water, cook the pasta until just tender, 2 to 3 minutes. Drain, and return to the pot.

3. Add the broth and peas to the pasta and toss well. Cover and let stand for 1 minute to allow the pasta to absorb some of the broth. Transfer to a warmed serving bowl, sprinkle with the chives and pepper, and toss again. Serve immediately.

NUTRITIONAL ANALYSIS PER SERVING (BASED ON 8 SERVINGS)

CALORIES: 200 (16 percent from protein, 74 percent from carbohydrate, 11 percent from fat) • PROTEIN: 8 grams • CARBOHYDRATE: 36 grams • FAT: 2 grams • CHOLESTEROL: 0 milligrams • SODIUM: 209 milligrams

ASPARAGUS AND RICOTTA PASTA

———

The second asparagus shows up in my market, I buy a pound or two for a binge (luckily, asparagus is low-fat as well as high-fiber). This is one of my favorite ways to use my favorite vegetable.

———

1 pound thin asparagus, tough stalks discarded
1 cup vegetable stock, preferably homemade (page 220)
1 teaspoon grated lemon zest
¼ teaspoon salt
¼ teaspoon freshly ground black pepper
1 pound freshly made or store-bought fresh cholesterol-free linguine
1 cup nonfat ricotta, at room temperature
2 tablespoons chopped fresh basil, chives, or parsley
6 tablespoons to ½ cup freshly grated Parmesan cheese

———

1. Trim the asparagus and cut into 1-inch lengths, separating the tender tips from the tougher bottom portions.

2. In a large nonstick skillet, bring the stock to a simmer. Add the asparagus bottoms and simmer, covered, 1 minute. Add the asparagus tips and cook, uncovered, until the asparagus is crisp-tender, about 2 more minutes. Stir in the lemon zest, salt, and pepper.

3. Meanwhile, in a large pot of boiling salted water, cook the pasta until just tender, 1 to 2 minutes. Drain and return to the pot.

4. Add the asparagus and broth to the pasta and toss. Transfer to a warmed serving bowl. Drop dollops of the ricotta over the top, then sprinkle with the basil. Toss again and serve, sprinkling each serving with 1 tablespoon Parmesan cheese.

NUTRITIONAL ANALYSIS PER SERVING (BASED ON 8 SERVINGS)

CALORIES: 239 (24 percent from protein, 61 percent from carbohydrate, 16 percent from fat) • PROTEIN: 14 grams • CARBOHYDRATE: 36 grams • FAT: 4 grams • CHOLESTEROL: 10 milligrams • SODIUM: 383 milligrams

MUSHROOM AND LEEK ORZO "RISOTTO"

Orzo is rice-shaped pasta, so it wasn't such a leap to orzo "risotto." Pasta is not always first boiled in water, and then dressed with a sauce, but is sometimes cooked directly in the sauce, as this recipe illustrates. Make it for good friends who will stand in the kitchen and share a glass of wine with you while you stir up your "risotto."

½ *ounce dried porcini mushrooms (about ½ cup)*
1 *cup boiling water*
4 *cups chicken stock, preferably homemade (page 212), or*
   low-sodium canned broth
2 *medium leeks, trimmed, chopped, and well rinsed*
2 *teaspoons olive oil*
8 *ounces (1 cup) dried orzo*
¼ *cup freshly grated imported Parmesan cheese*

1. Rinse the mushrooms under cold water to loosen the grit. Place in a small bowl, cover with the boiling water, and let stand until softened, 20 to 30 minutes.

2. Lift the mushrooms from the water, rinse again, and coarsely chop. Place the mushrooms in a medium bowl. Strain the soaking liquid through a paper towel–lined sieve to remove the grit, and reserve the liquid.

3. In a medium saucepan, bring the stock and the reserved mushroom liquid to a simmer over medium heat. Reduce the heat to very low and keep the liquid at a bare simmer.

4. In a large nonstick skillet, combine the leeks and ¼ cup of the simmering broth mixture. Bring to a simmer, cover, and cook until the leeks are very tender, about 10 minutes. Transfer to the bowl with the mushrooms and set aside.

(continued)

5. Wipe out the skillet with paper towels. Add the oil to the skillet and heat over medium heat. Add the orzo and cook, stirring often, until the orzo is lightly toasted, about 3 minutes. Stir in about ¾ cup of the simmering broth mixture. Reduce the heat to medium-low and simmer, stirring often, until the orzo has almost completely absorbed the stock, about 3 minutes. Continue stirring in the broth in ¾-cup additions, allowing each addition to be almost entirely absorbed before adding more and, cook until the pasta is just tender, about 20 minutes. (If the broth is gone before the pasta is tender, use boiling water until the desired tenderness is reached.)

6. Stir in the mushrooms and leeks and just heat through, about 1 minute. Transfer to individual bowls, sprinkle each serving with 1 tablespoon of the Parmesan cheese, and serve immediately.

NUTRITIONAL ANALYSIS PER SERVING

CALORIES: 344 (16 percent from protein, 67 percent from carbohydrate, 17 percent from fat) • PROTEIN: 14 grams • CARBOHYDRATE: 58 grams • FAT: 7 grams • CHOLESTEROL: 0 milligrams • SODIUM: 824 milligrams

The Asian Noodle Bowl

I grew up near San Francisco, and many Sunday afternoons, my parents would drive my brothers and me over to Chinatown. We'd stroll up and down the crowded streets all afternoon. Late in the day, Dad was always sure to pick up bean sprouts, water chestnuts, and Chinese egg noodles (and a certain type of sugared coconut chips that I still crave, but can't seem to find anymore). When we returned home, the entire family would go to work making chow mein. The boys would be responsible for meticulously slicing the celery, mushrooms, onions, and water chestnuts (the beginning of my career), but only Dad could fry the noodle pancake, which he could flip with a professionalism that would have made any Chinese chef envious.

While Chinese noodles are still popular, a whole new world of Asian pastas has exploded onto the culinary scene. This chapter shows how to use the different noodles available at your Asian grocer or supermarket. These pastas are not as exotic or esoteric as you may suspect—I can buy all of them at my neighborhood supermarket. Following are the noodles you'll find in these recipes.

Oriental egg noodles: Available dried and fresh. In order to keep within this book's low-fat guidelines, I usually prefer to use store-bought fresh cholesterol-free linguine as an excellent substitute. You can, of course, make your own from Classic Egg Pasta (page 34).

Oriental water noodles: Found dried, refrigerated, and frozen. The best, contain nothing more than flour and water. For a recipe, see page 37.

Rice noodles: Often called rice sticks. The thick rice sticks are also called *bahm pho,* and are often used for the popular Thai dish known as pad Thai. Thin rice sticks (*mai fun* or rice vermicelli) are used for stir-fries. Both types are purchased dried, then soaked briefly in warm water until supple, and drained.

Cellophane noodles: (also called bean threads or *sai fun*): Made from soybeans and come in small bundles that look like large rubber bands. They must be soaked in warm water until softened and drained. After soaking, they are practically transparent. They are used in many Asian cuisines, particularly Chinese and Korean.

KOREAN BEAN THREADS WITH BEEF AND VEGETABLES

MAKES 6 SERVINGS

While I was in Korea to teach a series of American cooking classes, *chapchae* became my favorite lunch. Maybe it's the contrasting textures that perk my appetite—slippery cellophane noodles, crisp-tender vegetables, and chewy slices of beef. Note that you have to soak the bean threads and mushrooms briefly, as well as marinate the beef, but once those easy tasks have been accomplished, you'll be sitting down to a bowl of *chapchae* in minutes.

---

6 dried shiitake (Chinese black) mushrooms
4 ounces cellophane noodles (also called bean threads or sai fun*)*
6 tablespoons low-sodium soy sauce
3 scallions, 1 finely chopped and 2 cut into thin diagonal slices
2 teaspoons sugar
2 garlic cloves, minced
6 ounces beef sirloin, well trimmed and cut into thin 2-inch shreds
1 tablespoon dark Asian sesame oil
¼ teaspoon freshly ground black pepper
1 tablespoon vegetable oil
1 large carrot, cut into very thin 2-inch shreds
1 small bunch watercress, trimmed and coarsely chopped

---

1. In a small bowl, soak the mushrooms in hot water to cover until softened, 20 to 40 minutes. In a large bowl, soak the bean threads in hot water to cover until just softened, about 20 minutes.

2. Meanwhile, in a medium bowl, mix 2 tablespoons of the soy sauce, the chopped scallion, 1 teaspoon of the sugar, and the garlic. Add the beef shreds and let marinate at room temperature for 20 minutes.

3. In a small bowl, mix the remaining ¼ cup soy sauce and 1 teaspoon sugar, the sesame oil, and pepper. Set aside.

(continued)

· THE ASIAN NOODLE BOWL ·

4. When the noodles are softened, drain well and set aside.

5. Drain the mushrooms, and remove and discard the stems. Cut the caps into ¼-inch-wide strips.

6. In a nonstick skillet or wok, heat the vegetable oil over high heat. Add the beef with its marinade and stir-fry for 1 minute. Add the carrot, sliced scallions, and the mushrooms and stir-fry for 1 minute. Add the watercress and stir-fry for 1 minute. Add the drained noodles and the soy–sesame oil mixture, and stir-fry, mixing well, just until the bean threads are heated through and well coated, about 1 minute. Transfer to a serving bowl and serve hot, warm, or at room temperature.

Note: While these are the classic vegetables for *chapchae*, you can experiment with others, such as broccoli florets, thinly sliced celery or onions, or bean sprouts. You can also substitute 2 cups of thinly shredded spinach for the watercress.

NUTRITIONAL ANALYSIS PER SERVING

CALORIES: 192 (16 percent from protein, 50 percent from carbohydrate, 35 percent from fat) • PROTEIN: 7 grams • CARBOHYDRATE: 23 grams • FAT: 7 grams • CHOLESTEROL: 19 milligrams • SODIUM: 625 milligrams

STIR-FRIED THAI RICE NOODLES WITH SHRIMP AND TOFU

MAKES 6 SERVINGS

———

Many popular Thai dishes are easy to make at home, once you find the ingredients. Pad Thai is a classic, with tender rice noodles in a tangy sauce accented by shrimp, bean sprouts, and a dusting of chopped peanuts.

———

8 ounces thick rice noodles (also called bahm pho)
2 tablespoons low-sodium soy sauce
2 tablespoons low-sodium Worcestershire sauce
¼ cup water
2 tablespoons ketchup
2 tablespoons sugar
1 tablespoon rice vinegar
2 tablespoons vegetable oil
8 ounces medium shrimp, peeled and deveined
4 garlic cloves, minced
4 scallions, finely chopped
2 medium shallots, minced (or 3 additional scallions, finely chopped)
⅓ cup liquid egg substitute or 1 large egg plus 2 large egg whites, beaten together
2 cups fresh bean sprouts
¼ cup chopped fresh cilantro
3 tablespoons chopped unsalted dry-roasted peanuts
Crushed hot red pepper
1 lime, cut into 6 wedges

———

1. In a large bowl, soak the rice sticks in hot water to cover until softened and supple, 10 to 15 minutes. Drain well and set aside.

2. In a small bowl, mix the soy sauce, Worcestershire sauce, water, ketchup, sugar, and rice vinegar. Set aside.

(continued)

· THE ASIAN NOODLE BOWL ·

3. In a large nonstick skillet or wok, heat the oil over high heat. Add the shrimp and stir-fry just until pink and firm, about 2 minutes. Remove the shrimp with a slotted spoon and set aside.

4. Add the garlic, scallions, and shallots to the skillet and stir-fry for 30 seconds. Add the egg substitute and stir until barely set, about 15 seconds. Add the noodles and soy sauce mixture, and cook, stirring often, until the liquid has been absorbed by the noodles, about 2 minutes. Remove from heat and stir in the shrimp and bean sprouts.

5. Transfer to individual plates, and sprinkle each serving with the chopped cilantro and peanuts. Serve immediately, accompanied by bowls of red pepper flakes and the lime wedges for seasoning.

NUTRITIONAL ANALYSIS PER SERVING

CALORIES: 322 (17 percent from protein, 55 percent from carbohydrates, 28 percent from fat) • PROTEIN: 13 grams • CARBOHYDRATE: 45 grams • FAT: 10 grams • CHOLESTEROL: 58 milligrams • SODIUM: 576 milligrams

BURMESE CURRIED RICE NOODLES

MAKES 6 SERVINGS

————

Thin shreds of pork, an assortment of colorful vegetables, and bright yellow curry sauce make these noodles a visually exciting and mouth-watering meal. Those with tender palates may choose to reduce the amount of curry powder, but this is supposed to be a highly seasoned dish.

————

6 dried shiitake (Chinese black) mushrooms

8 ounces thin rice noodles (also called rice vermicelli or mai fun)

⅓ cup chicken stock, preferably homemade (page 212), or low-sodium canned broth, or more as necessary

3 tablespoons low-sodium soy sauce

1 tablespoon curry powder, preferably Madras-style

1 tablespoon brown sugar

1 tablespoon vegetable oil

8 ounces pork tenderloin, well trimmed of any fat and cut into thin 2-inch shreds

1 small onion, halved lengthwise and cut into thin half-moons

2 medium celery ribs, cut diagonally into ¼-inch-thick slices

4 ounces snow peas, trimmed, strings removed, and cut diagonally into ¼-inch-wide strips

1 small red bell pepper, stemmed, seeded, and cut into ¼-inch-thick strips

1 tablespoon grated fresh ginger

1 scallion, chopped

————

1. In a small bowl, soak the mushrooms in hot water to cover until soft-ened, 20 to 40 minutes. Drain, cut off and discard the stems, and cut the caps into ¼-inch-wide strips.

2. Meanwhile, in a large bowl, soak the rice sticks in lukewarm water to cover until just softened but still slightly resilient, about 15 minutes. Drain well and set aside.

(continued)

3. In a small bowl, mix the chicken stock, soy sauce, curry powder, and brown sugar. Set aside.

4. In a large nonstick skillet or wok, heat the oil. Add the pork shreds and stir-fry until the pork loses its raw color, 1 to 2 minutes. Add the onion, celery, snow peas, red bell pepper, ginger, and scallion and stir-fry until the vegetables are just crisp-tender, 1 to 2 minutes. Stir in the soy sauce mixture, then add the drained noodles and stir-fry just until the noodles are well coated with the sauce. (If the noodles seem dry, add more chicken broth.) Transfer to a warmed serving bowl and serve immediately.

NUTRITIONAL ANALYSIS PER SERVING

CALORIES: 257 (19 percent from protein, 67 percent from carbohydrate, 15 percent from fat) • PROTEIN: 12 grams • CARBOHYDRATE: 42 grams • FAT: 4 grams • CHOLESTEROL: 27 milligrams • SODIUM: 373 milligrams

VEGETABLE AND NOODLE STIR-FRY

MAKES 6 SERVINGS

———

Here's the way to enjoy a favorite Chinese restaurant dish with a minimum of fat and no MSG. You will need a very large nonstick skillet or a nonstick wok for this dish.

———

1 pound freshly made or store-bought fresh cholesterol-free linguine
½ cup chicken stock, preferably homemade (page 212), or
   low-sodium canned broth
3 tablespoons low-sodium soy sauce
1 tablespoon rice vinegar
1 tablespoon dry sherry
1 tablespoon unsulphured molasses
Nonstick vegetable cooking spray
3 scallions, chopped
2 tablespoons grated fresh ginger
1 garlic clove, minced
¼ teaspoon crushed hot red pepper
2 cups shredded Chinese (Nappa) cabbage
6 large fresh mushrooms, sliced
1 medium celery rib, cut diagonally into ¼-inch-thick slices
1 medium carrot, cut diagonally into ⅛-inch-thick slices
½ cup sliced drained canned water chestnuts
2 cups fresh bean sprouts

———

1. In a large pot of boiling salted water, cook the noodles until barely tender, 1 to 2 minutes. (Do not overcook; they will cook further when stir-fried.) Drain, rinse under cold water, and drain again. Place the noodles in a bowl, cover with cold water, and set aside.

2. In a small bowl, mix the stock, soy sauce, vinegar, sherry, and molasses. Set aside.

(continued)

———

· THE ASIAN NOODLE BOWL ·

3. Spray a very large (14-inch) nonstick skillet or wok with nonstick cooking spray and heat over high heat. Add the scallions, ginger, garlic, and hot pepper and stir-fry until fragrant, about 30 seconds. Add the cabbage, mushrooms, celery, carrot, water chestnuts, and ¼ cup of the soy sauce mixture. Cover and cook until the vegetables are crisp-tender, about 2 minutes. Transfer the vegetables to a dish.

4. Drain the noodles well. Respray the skillet with nonstick vegetable spray and reheat over high heat. Add the noodles and the remaining soy sauce mixture to the skillet. Stir-fry for 30 seconds. Add the bean sprouts and reserved vegetables and stir-fry until the bean sprouts are heated through but still crisp, about 1 minute. Transfer to a serving platter and serve immediately.

NUTRITIONAL ANALYSIS PER SERVING

CALORIES: 286 (15 percent from protein, 75 percent from carbohydrate, 9 percent from fat) • PROTEIN: 11 grams • CARBOHYDRATE: 54 grams • FAT: 3 grams • CHOLESTEROL: 0 milligrams • SODIUM: 402 milligrams

EGG NOODLES WITH PEKING TURKEY AND VEGETABLE SAUCE

MAKES 8 FIRST-COURSE SERVINGS

———

Traditional Peking meat sauce, usually made with ground pork, is a rich foil for smooth-as-silk fresh egg noodles. My version is lightened with ground turkey and chopped vegetables, but the flavor is far from diminished. While you can certainly enjoy it in larger portions, I prefer this as a first course, followed by a vegetable stir-fry and chilled fresh fruit for dessert. Brown bean sauce is made from soy beans (not black beans), and can be found in Chinese markets and many supermarkets.

———

· MR. PASTA'S HEALTHY PASTA COOKBOOK ·

⅓ cup brown bean sauce (often labeled sauce des legumes)

2 tablespoons Scotch or dry sherry

2 teaspoons unsulphured molasses

¼ teaspoon crushed hot red pepper

½ pound ground turkey

1 medium carrot, finely chopped

1 medium celery rib, finely chopped

2 scallions, chopped

1 tablespoon grated fresh ginger

2 garlic cloves, minced

½ cup chicken stock, preferably homemade (page 212), or low-sodium canned broth

1 pound freshly made or store-bought fresh cholesterol-free egg noodles

2 teaspoons dark Asian sesame oil

2 cups fresh bean sprouts

---

1. In a small bowl, whisk together the bean sauce, Scotch, molasses, and red pepper flakes until smooth. Set aside.

2. In a large nonstick skillet, combine the ground turkey, carrot, and celery and cook over medium heat, breaking up the turkey with a wooden spoon, until the turkey loses its pink color, about 5 minutes. Add the scallions, ginger, and garlic and stir-fry for 30 seconds. Stir in the chicken stock and bean sauce mixture, reduce the heat to medium-low, and simmer until the liquid has evaporated by half, about 5 minutes. Keep warm.

3. Meanwhile, in a large pot of boiling salted water, cook the noodles until barely tender, 1 to 2 minutes. Drain well and return to the pot.

4. Toss the noodles with the sesame oil, then add the warm meat sauce and toss well. Transfer to individual bowls, top with the bean sprouts, and serve immediately.

NUTRITIONAL ANALYSIS PER SERVING

CALORIES: 272 (17 percent from protein, 60 percent from carbohydrate, 20 percent from fat) • PROTEIN: 12 grams • CARBOHYDRATE: 40 grams • FAT: 6 grams • CHOLESTEROL: 11 milligrams • SODIUM: 86 milligrams

· THE ASIAN NOODLE BOWL ·

VIETNAMESE BEEF AND CELLOPHANE NOODLE SOUP

MAKES 4 SERVINGS

——

This fragrant soup is especially refreshing thanks to the fresh taste and texture of the barely cooked spinach and sprouts. It also happens to illustrate the important low-fat cooking principle using a little meat to go a long way.

——

5 ounces boneless beef sirloin, well trimmed of any fat
2 ounces cellophane noodles (also called bean threads or sai fun)
4 cups chicken stock, preferably homemade (page 212), or
   low-sodium canned broth
1 3-inch length of lemongrass, from the root end, chopped
   (page 20)
1 slice fresh ginger, about the size of a quarter
1 garlic clove, crushed
1 tablespoon low-sodium soy sauce
1 tablespoon low-sodium Worcestershire sauce
2 cups fresh spinach, washed, stemmed, and coarsely chopped
2 ounces fresh bean sprouts
1 scallion, thinly sliced
¼ cup finely chopped fresh cilantro
Crushed hot red pepper

——

1. Place the steak in the freezer until partially frozen, about 30 minutes. Using a sharp knife, cut on the diagonal across the grain into very thin slices. Set aside.

2. Meanwhile, in a large bowl, soak the cellophane noodles in hot water to cover until just softened, 15 to 20 minutes. Drain and set aside.

3. In a medium saucepan, combine the stock, lemongrass, ginger, and garlic and bring to a simmer over medium-high heat. Reduce the heat to low and simmer for 10 minutes.

4. Using a perforated spoon, scoop the solids out of the stock and discard. Add the beef slices, soy sauce, and Worcestershire sauce and cook just until the beef loses its raw look, about 1 minute.

5. To serve, divide the noodles, spinach, bean sprouts, scallion, and cilantro among four individual serving bowls. Ladle the hot soup into the bowls. Serve immediately, allowing each guest to season to taste with red pepper flakes.

NUTRITIONAL ANALYSIS PER SERVING

CALORIES: 177 (30 percent from protein, 45 percent from carbohydrate, 25 percent from fat) • PROTEIN: 13 grams • CARBOHYDRATE: 20 grams • FAT: 5 grams • CHOLESTEROL: 29 milligrams • SODIUM: 431 milligrams

---

THAI CHICKEN-BASIL SAUCE
WITH LINGUINE

MAKES 4 SERVINGS

———

Many Bangkok market food stalls serve this highly seasoned ground chicken sauce on fresh noodles, all tossed with a good handful of their native anise-scented holy basil. Holy basil is quite different from our familiar Mediterranean basil. While Thai cooks may disagree, I think that the American garden variety basil only makes this delicious dish a little different from the traditional version, neither better nor worse. Of course, if you have a Thai market nearby, use holy basil.

———

Nonstick vegetable cooking spray
1/2 pound ground chicken
1 medium carrot, cut into 1/4-inch dice
1 medium zucchini, well scrubbed and cut into 1/4-inch dice
4 shallots, minced
1 fresh hot chile pepper, seeded and minced (or to taste)
1 tablespoon grated fresh ginger
2 garlic cloves, minced
3/4 cup chicken stock, preferably homemade (page 212), or
    low-sodium canned broth
1 tablespoon low-sodium soy sauce
1 tablespoon low-sodium Worcestershire sauce
1 tablespoon fresh lime juice
1 teaspoon sugar
1/2 cup packed coarsely chopped basil leaves
Salt, to taste
1 pound freshly made or store-bought fresh cholesterol-free linguine

———

1. Spray a nonstick skillet with nonstick vegetable spray. Add the ground chicken, carrot, zucchini, shallots, chile pepper, ginger, and garlic. Cook over medium heat, stirring to break up the chicken with a spoon, until the chicken loses its pink color, about 5 minutes. Drain off any liquid.

2. Add the stock, soy sauce, Worcestershire sauce, lime juice, and sugar and bring to a boil. Reduce the heat to low and simmer for 5 minutes. Stir in the basil leaves and cook until the leaves are wilted, about 1 minute. Season with salt, to taste. Keep warm.

3. Meanwhile, in a large pot of boiling salted water, cook the pasta until just tender, 1 to 2 minutes. Drain well and return to the pot.

4. Add the sauce and toss well. Transfer to a warmed serving bowl and serve immediately.

NUTRITIONAL ANALYSIS PER SERVING (BASED ON 4 SERVINGS)
CALORIES: 342 (30 percent from protein, 57 percent from carbohydrate, 13 percent from fat) •
PROTEIN: 24 grams • CARBOHYDRATE: 46 grams • FAT: 4 grams • CHOLESTEROL: 84 milligrams
• SODIUM: 736 milligrams

Simmer Down: Pasta Soups

Soups are great for filling up and for slimming down. But pasta soups, with their extra sustenance, are really rib-sticking, and keep hunger pangs at bay.

I've used quite a collection of soup pastas here. Many of them look as if they came from a colony of elves—tiny bow ties, thimbles, tubes, or stars. Minuscule these soup pastas may be, but don't undercook them. They take about ten minutes to get good and tender. This is one type of pasta that isn't served al dente.

First-class homemade stocks make first-class homemade soups. Canned broths are a convenience, but just that—they don't really compare to fresh. I have included recipes for chicken, fish, and vegetable stocks that can be used as the starting point for a delicious soup or as an ingredient in other recipes. I have a freezer full of stocks—and pasta sauces—that I use almost every day. It's best to freeze stocks in one- or two-cup containers so you don't have to defrost more than you need.

Pasta soups tend to thicken upon standing, as the noodles soak up the broth. If you have leftovers, plan on adding more broth or water to bring the soup back to its original consistency.

MEXICAN TOMATO-NOODLE SOUP

MAKES 6 TO 8 SERVINGS

I learned to make this simple but satisfying noodle-packed soup when I was a language student in Guadalajara. When it is prepared with pre-made broth, parents will find this a quick and easy way to serve homemade soup to the kids during their lunch hour, but the youngsters may prefer the soup without the chile pepper. The chicken stock in this recipe can be used in any dish in this book that calls for chicken stock.

HOMEMADE CHICKEN STOCK

3 pounds chicken backs
1 medium onion, chopped
1 medium carrot, chopped
1 medium celery rib with leaves, chopped
2½ quarts water
4 sprigs parsley
½ teaspoon dried thyme
1 bay leaf
½ teaspoon salt
¼ teaspoon black peppercorns

1 tablespoon olive oil
4 ounces dried fideos *(thin coiled egg noodles)*
1 28-ounce can tomatoes in juice, drained
1 medium onion, quartered
1 fresh hot chile pepper, such as jalepeño, seeded and chopped
2 garlic cloves, crushed
7 cups chicken broth, preferably homemade (see above), or use low-
     sodium canned broth
¼ teaspoon freshly ground black pepper
6 tablespoons nonfat sour cream alternative
Lime wedges for garnish

1. Make the chicken stock: Spray a large pot with nonstick vegetable spray and place over medium-high heat. Add the chicken backs, skin side down, and cook until the skin is browned, about 5 minutes, then turn and brown the other side. Add the onion, carrot, and celery, cover, and cook until the vegetables are softened, about 10 minutes. Add the water and bring to a boil, skimming off any foam that rises to the surface. Add the parsley, thyme, bay leaf, salt, and peppercorns. Reduce the heat to low and simmer until reduced to about 2 quarts, 2½ to 3 hours.

2. Strain the stock into a large bowl. Let stand 5 minutes, then skim off any fat on the surface. (It is easiest to remove the fat if the stock is chilled. Cool the stock to room temperature, then cover and refrigerate until chilled, at least 4 hours. Lift off the hardened fat and discard. The stock can be prepared ahead, covered, and refrigerated for up to 3 days or frozen for up to 2 months.)

3. In a large nonstick skillet, heat the olive oil over medium heat. Add the noodle nests and cook, turning once, until lightly browned on both sides, about 2 minutes. Using tongs, transfer to paper towels to drain. Set the skillet aside.

4. In a blender, process the drained tomatoes, onion, chile pepper, and garlic until smooth. Pour into the skillet and bring to a boil over medium heat. Cover partially (the mixture will splatter as it cooks) and boil, stirring often to avoid scorching, until thickened and reduced by about one third, 8 to 10 minutes.

5. Transfer the tomato mixture to a soup pot. Stir in the chicken stock, browned noodles, and the pepper. Bring to a simmer, reduce the heat to low, and simmer gently until the noodles are very soft, 15 to 20 minutes.

6. Ladle the hot soup into individual bowls, and top each serving with a dollop of sour cream. Pass lime wedges for squeezing into the soup as a seasoning.

NUTRITIONAL ANALYSIS PER SERVING (BASED ON 8 SERVINGS)
CALORIES: 91 (19 percent from protein, 52 percent from carbohydrate, 29 percent from fat) •
PROTEIN: 5 grams • CARBOHYDRATE: 12 grams • FAT: 3 grams • CHOLESTEROL: 4 milligrams •
SODIUM: 794 milligrams

FISH AND PASTA SOUP NIÇOISE

———

Southern France, one of my favorite vacation spots, is famous for its fish soups. There this heady, saffron-scented soup is usually served as a first course, but most Americans will find it substantial enough for an entrée. Use at least two kinds of firm-fleshed, nonoily fish for depth of flavor. I suggest buying about three pounds of whole fish, such as sea bass, scrod, rock cod, red snapper, or porgy. Ask the fishmonger to fillet the fish; use the bones (you'll get about one pound) for the stock, and the pound or so of fillets for the soup. You may substitute four cups bottled clam juice and three and a half cups water for the fish stock, if you wish, but in that case, season the soup to taste with salt at the *end* of the cooking time, as bottled clam juice can be salty.

———

FISH STOCK

Approximately 1 pound fish bones with heads (gills removed),
  well rinsed
7 cups cold water
1 cup dry white wine
1 medium onion, chopped
1 celery rib, chopped
1 garlic clove, crushed
4 sprigs parsley
1/2 teaspoon dried thyme
1 bay leaf
1/8 teaspoon black peppercorns

1 tablespoon olive oil
2 medium leeks, trimmed, chopped, and well rinsed
1 medium onion, chopped
1/2 small fennel bulb, trimmed, cored, and chopped (about 1 cup)
1 medium celery rib with leaves, chopped
2 garlic cloves, minced
1 28-ounce can tomatoes in juice, drained and chopped

1 teaspoon dried oregano
1 teaspoon dried thyme
1 bay leaf
½ teaspoon salt
¼ teaspoon crushed hot red pepper
½ cup dried tiny soup pasta, such as tubetti or orzo
1 pound firm-fleshed, nonoily fish fillets, skinned and cut into
   1-inch pieces
½ teaspoon crushed saffron threads
6 tablespoons freshly grated imported Parmesan cheese

---

1. Make the fish stock: In a large pot, combine the fish bones, water, wine, onion, celery, and garlic. Bring to a boil over high heat, skimming off any foam that rises to the surface. Add the parsley, thyme, bay leaf, and peppercorns, reduce the heat to low, and simmer, uncovered, for 30 minutes. Strain the stock, add water, if needed, to measure 7½ cups. (The stock can be prepared up to 2 days ahead, cooled to room temperature, covered, and refrigerated.)

2. Heat the oil in a large pot over medium heat. Add the leeks, onion, fennel, celery, and garlic and cook, covered, until the onion is softened, about 5 minutes. Stir in the fish stock, tomatoes, oregano, thyme, bay leaf, salt, and crushed red pepper and bring to a boil. Reduce the heat to low and simmer, partially covered, for 45 minutes.

3. Stir the pasta into the soup and cook for 5 minutes. Add the fish and saffron and cook until the pasta is tender and the fish is firm, about 5 minutes. Ladle into soup bowls and serve hot, sprinkling each serving with 1 tablespoon of the Parmesan cheese.

NUTRITIONAL ANALYSIS PER SERVING

CALORIES: 401 (27 percent from protein, 50 percent from carbohydrate, 16 percent from fat) • PROTEIN: 28 grams • CARBOHYDRATE: 51 grams • FAT: 7 grams • CHOLESTEROL: 41 milligrams • SODIUM: 397 milligrams

QUICK PASTA AND BEAN SOUP

MAKES 8 TO 10 SERVINGS

Few soups warm the body and spirit like *pasta e fagioli,* a rustic dish from the Veneto region of northern Italy. You can use almost any kind of bean to personalize your soup, but the classic is the cranberry bean, also called the Roman bean. While I have sometimes made this with freshly cooked beans and sometimes with canned beans, I find canned beans quicker—and the flavor doesn't suffer in the least.

---

1 tablespoon olive oil
2 ounces Canadian bacon, cut into ¼-inch cubes
1 large onion, finely chopped
2 celery ribs, finely chopped
2 carrots, finely chopped
4 garlic cloves, minced
4 cups chicken stock, preferably homemade (page 212), or
   low-sodium canned broth
4 cups water
2 16-ounce cans cranberry (Roman) beans, drained and rinsed
1 16-ounce can tomatoes in juice, drained and chopped
2 tablespoons tomato paste
2 teaspoons dried oregano
2 teaspoons dried basil
1 teaspoon dried rosemary
½ teaspoon salt
½ teaspoon freshly ground black pepper
⅔ cup dried tiny soup pasta, such as tubetti

---

1. In a large pot, heat the oil over medium heat. Add the Canadian bacon, onion, celery, carrots, and garlic. Cover and cook until the onions are softened, about 5 minutes. Stir in the stock, water, drained beans, tomatoes, tomato paste, oregano, basil, rosemary, salt, and pepper. Bring to a boil, reduce the heat to low, and simmer, partially covered, for 20 minutes.

2. Stir the pasta into the soup and cook until tender, about 10 minutes. Using a potato masher or a large spoon, crush the solids in the pot until the soup reaches a creamy consistency. Serve hot. (The soup can be prepared up to 3 days ahead, cooled to room temperature, covered, and refrigerated. It will thicken upon standing, so dilute it with water or broth to the desired consistency when reheating.)

NUTRITIONAL ANALYSIS PER SERVING (BASED ON 10 SERVINGS)
CALORIES: 166 (20 percent from protein, 64 percent from carbohydrate, 16 percent from fat) •
PROTEIN: 8 grams • CARBOHYDRATE: 27 grams • FAT: 3 grams • CHOLESTEROL: 3 milligrams •
SODIUM: 766 milligrams

VEGETABLE, PESTO, AND PASTA SOUP

MAKES 8 TO 10 SERVINGS

Some dishes just aren't worth making unless you make *a lot*. I think vegetable soup falls into that category, especially this South of France–inspired garden-patch-in-a-pot. It's called *pistou*, which is French for "pesto," as the basil condiment is as popular along the Côte d'Azur as it is in its native Liguria. You can use other vegetables—for the French certainly do: Yellow or green beans, peas, yellow squash, and asparagus all have been in one pistou or another.

2 teaspoons olive oil
3 sweet Italian turkey sausages (about 7 ounces), casings removed
   and crumbled
2 medium leeks, trimmed, finely chopped, and well rinsed
2 medium celery ribs, finely chopped
2 medium carrots, finely chopped
1 medium zucchini, well scrubbed and finely chopped
2 garlic cloves, minced
4 cups chicken stock, preferably homemade (page 212), or
   low-sodium canned broth
4 cups water
3 medium new potatoes, well scrubbed and cut into 1/2-inch cubes
1 16-ounce can tomatoes in juice, drained and chopped
1/4 teaspoon salt
1/4 teaspoon freshly ground black pepper
2/3 cup dried orzo
1/2 cup Lean Pesto (page 88)

1. In a large nonstick skillet, heat the oil over medium heat. Add the turkey sausage, leeks, celery, carrots, zucchini, and garlic, and cook, stirring often with a spoon to break up the sausage, until the vegetables are softened, 8 to 10 minutes. Transfer to a large soup pot.

2. Stir in the chicken stock, water, potatoes, tomatoes, salt, and pepper, and bring to a boil over high heat. Reduce the heat to low and simmer, partially covered, until the potatoes are just tender, 15 to 20 minutes. Stir in the pasta, increase the heat to high, and cook until the pasta is tender, about 6 minutes.

3. Ladle the soup into individual soup bowls, topping each serving with a dollop of the pesto to be stirred into the soup by your guests.

Note: I like to use the rice-shaped orzo in this soup because it's easy to eat with a spoon. But pistou is a great way to use up any leftover uncooked pasta. Almost every recipe for pistou recommends a different pasta shape—strips of fettuccine or vermicelli, penne, shells. So stir half a cup or so of whatever you have into the simmering soup and cook until tender.

NUTRITIONAL ANALYSIS PER SERVING (BASED ON 10 SERVINGS)
CALORIES: 190 (19 percent from protein, 64 percent from carbohydrate, 18 percent from fat) • PROTEIN: 9 grams • CARBOHYDRATE: 31 grams • FAT: 4 grams • CHOLESTEROL: 15 milligrams • SODIUM: 653 milligrams

GARLIC-VEGETABLE SOUP WITH WHOLE WHEAT NOODLES

MAKES 8 SERVINGS

Garlic is mellowed when long-simmered, lending an elusive savory note to this soup. The vegetable stock below can be used for any recipe in this book that specifies vegetable stock—so long as you do not squeeze the garlic flesh back into the stock, and strain it before using. Like chicken stock, it freezes beautifully, and it is far better than any instant vegetable broths you may purchase at a natural foods store.

HEADY VEGETABLE STOCK

2 medium onions, chopped
2 celery ribs with leaves, chopped
2 medium carrots, chopped
1 large baking potato, well scrubbed and chopped
1 head garlic, halved crosswise
1 teaspoon salt
1/2 teaspoon dried thyme
1 bay leaf
1/4 teaspoon freshly ground black pepper
3 quarts water

8 ounces dried whole wheat fettuccine (available in natural foods stores and many supermarkets)

1. Make the vegetable stock: In a large pot, combine all of the stock ingredients and bring to a boil over high heat. Reduce the heat to low and simmer, partially covered, for 3 hours. Using tongs remove the garlic halves, and cool slightly.

2. Squeeze the soft garlic pulp onto a small plate, and mash with a fork into a puree. Stir back into the stock, and bring the stock back to the boil. Add the pasta and cook until it is tender, about 7 minutes. Ladle into soup bowls and serve immediately.

NUTRITIONAL ANALYSIS PER SERVING

CALORIES: 153 (14 percent from protein, 83 percent from carbohydrate, 3 percent from fat) • PROTEIN: 6 grams • CARBOHYDRATE: 34 grams • FAT: less than 1 gram • CHOLESTEROL: 0 milligram • SODIUM: 298 milligrams

VINEYARD MINESTRONE

MAKES 10 SERVINGS

Many has been the winter afternoon that I've simmered up a big batch of this minestrone, which gets an extra dimension from a good dose of red wine. After I've warmed up with a steaming bowl, I freeze the remainder ready for a quick lunch or to serve to unexpected guests.

1 medium onion, chopped
2 carrots, cut into ¼-inch pieces
2 celery ribs, cut into ¼-inch pieces
1 zucchini, cut into ¼-inch pieces
1 red bell pepper, cut into ¼-inch pieces
2 garlic cloves, minced
5 cups chicken stock, preferably homemade (page 212), or
    low-sodium canned broth
4 cups water
1 cup red wine
1 28-ounce can tomatoes in juice, drained and chopped
2 teaspoons dried basil
1 teaspoon dried marjoram
1 16-ounce can white kidney beans, drained
2 cups shredded Savoy cabbage
½ cup dried tiny soup pasta, such as tubetti
½ cup freshly grated imported Parmesan cheese

1. In a large pot, combine the onion, carrots, celery, zucchini, bell pepper, garlic, stock, tomatoes, water, red wine, basil, and marjoram. Bring to a boil over high heat. Reduce the heat to medium-low and simmer, partially covered, for 1 hour.

2. Add the beans and cabbage and cook until the cabbage is tender, about 10 minutes. Stir in the pasta and cook, uncovered, until tender, about 10 minutes. Ladle the soup into soup bowls and serve immediately, sprinkling each serving with Parmesan cheese.

NUTRITIONAL ANALYSIS PER SERVING
CALORIES 154 (20 percent from protein, 56 percent from carbohydrate, 15 percent from fat) • PROTEIN: 8 grams • CARBOHYDRATE: 24 grams • FAT: 3 grams • CHOLESTEROL: 4 milligrams • SODIUM: 629 milligrams

---

ITALIAN SAUSAGE AND PEPPERS SOUP

MAKES 8 SERVINGS

Sausage and peppers is an Italian couple as stellar as Loren and Mastroianni. (Ah, Sophia, who once said, "Everything you see, I owe to spaghetti.") Italian turkey sausages have less fat and calories than their pork counterparts, but they are not diet food. Keep your portions to three ounces or below to stay within reasonable fat guidelines.

---

12 ounces sweet Italian turkey sausages
3½ cups chicken stock, preferably homemade (page 212), or low-sodium canned broth
1 large onion, chopped
2 red bell peppers, stemmed, seeded, and chopped
2 green bell peppers, stemmed, seeded, and chopped
2 garlic cloves, minced
3 cups water
½ teaspoon dried oregano
¼ teaspoon salt
¼ teaspoon freshly ground black pepper
½ cup dried tiny soup pasta, such as tubetti

(continued)

1. Prick the sausages all over with a fork and place in a medium nonstick skillet. Add 2 cups water, bring to a simmer over medium-high heat, and cook, turning occasionally, until the water has evaporated and the sausages are browned, about 15 minutes. Transfer the sausages to a plate, and let cool.

2. Remove the casings and slice the sausages into ½-inch-thick rounds. Set aside.

3. Meanwhile, in a large pot, combine ½ cup of the stock, the onion, green and red peppers, and garlic and bring to a simmer over medium-low heat. Cover and cook until the peppers are very tender, about 30 minutes.

4. Add the remaining 3 cups stock, the water, oregano, salt, and pepper and simmer, uncovered, 10 minutes. Add the reserved turkey sausages and the pasta and continue to simmer until the pasta is cooked, about 10 minutes. Ladle into individual serving bowls and serve immediately.

NUTRITIONAL ANALYSIS PER SERVING

CALORIES: 158 (28 percent from protein, 50 percent from carbohydrate, 22 percent from fat) • PROTEIN: 11 grams • CARBOHYDRATE: 20 grams • FAT: 4 grams • CHOLESTEROL: 27 milligrams • SODIUM: 732 milligrams

SAN FRANCISCO CIO-PASTA

MAKES 6 SERVINGS

Cioppino is the fish stew that San Francisco made famous. Most Golden Gate cooks serve it as a soupy-stew, but I like to spoon it over linguine as a pasta entrée. Make the tomato–red wine sauce well ahead so last-minute attention is minimized.

1 tablespoon olive oil
1 medium onion, chopped
1 medium celery rib with leaves, chopped
1 medium green bell pepper, stemmed, seeded, and chopped
2 garlic cloves, minced
1 cup red wine
4 cups fish stock (page 214) or 2 cups each bottled clam juice and water
1 28-ounce can tomatoes in juice, drained and pureed in a food processor or blender
1/2 cup chopped fresh parsley
2 tablespoons tomato paste
1 teaspoon dried basil
1 teaspoon dried oregano
1 teaspoon dried thyme
1/4 teaspoon crushed hot red pepper
Nonstick vegetable cooking spray
1 pound sea bass fillets, skinned and cut into 1-inch pieces
8 ounces medium shrimp, peeled and deveined
8 ounces small bay scallops
1/4 teaspoon salt
1/4 teaspoon freshly ground black pepper
1 pound freshly made or store-bought fresh cholesterol-free linguine
18 small hard-shell clams, well scrubbed and soaked (see page 151)

(continued)

1. In a large nonreactive pot, heat the oil over medium heat. Add the onion, celery, bell pepper, and garlic, cover, and cook, stirring often, until the onions are softened, about 5 minutes. Add the red wine, bring to a boil over high heat, and cook until the wine is reduced to ¼ cup, about 5 minutes. Stir in the fish stock, tomatoes, parsley, tomato paste, basil, oregano, thyme, and crushed red pepper, and bring to a simmer. Reduce the heat to low and simmer, partially covered, until the sauce has thickened, about 2 hours. Keep warm. (The sauce can be prepared up to 4 hours ahead and set aside at room temperature. Return to a simmer before proceeding.)

2. Spray a large nonstick skillet with nonstick cooking spray and place over medium-high heat. Add the sea bass, shrimp, and scallops and season with the salt and pepper. Cook, turning occasionally, just until the shrimp turn pink, about 3 minutes. Add the seafood to the tomato sauce, and transfer the cioppino to a warmed soup tureen.

3. Meanwhile, in a large pot of boiling salted water, cook the pasta until just tender, 1 to 2 minutes. Drain, and return to the empty pot. Add 1 cup of the cioppino and toss well, then transfer to a warmed serving bowl.

4. To serve, bring the cioppino and the pasta to the table. Transfer the pasta to individual bowls, ladle the cioppino on top, and serve immediately.

NUTRITIONAL ANALYSIS PER SERVING

CALORIES: 496 (33 percent from protein, 47 percent from carbohydrate, 14 percent from fat) • PROTEIN: 41 grams • CARBOHYDRATE: 58 grams • FAT: 8 grams • CHOLESTEROL: 109 milligrams • SODIUM: 879 milligrams

Pasta in the Shade: Pasta Salads

During my years as a caterer, there was rarely a party where I didn't serve some kind of pasta salad. Pasta salads are perfect for large groups, because everyone loves them, they're colorful, and they are easy to make ahead.

However, making pasta salads in advance demands one important piece of advice. As the salad sits, the pasta soaks up the dressing. If the salad has been refrigerated for more than an hour, the seasonings will need to be adjusted to compensate for the pasta's sponge-like character. My method is to toss the pasta and other ingredients with only half of the dressing when I put the salad together. Then the salad can be refrigerated for up to one day. When ready to serve, refresh the salad with the remaining dressing and re-season with a bit of salt and pepper.

Also, you always want to avoid overcooking pasta, but this admonition is doubly important when making pasta salad. The dressing will soften the pasta as it stands.

All of the salads in this chapter feature low-fat dressings. Better yet, most of the dressings can be prepared on their own and used to dress your everyday green salads (these luscious, slimmed-down dressings have their own subrecipes so they're easy to locate). Try Citrus-Mint Vinaigrette, Banana Curry Dressing, Cucumber-Cilantro Dressing, Gingery Peanut Dressing, Tomato-Sherry Dressing, and Cilantro-Tomatillo Pesto. All will keep, refrigerated, for up to three days.

ORZO "TABBOULEH"

MAKES 8 TO 10 SERVINGS

Tabbouleh is a Middle Eastern salad of bulgur, lots and lots of parsley, chunks of cucumber and tomato, and a sprinkling of mint. I like to substitute rice-shaped orzo pasta for the bulgur. This makes a large batch, perfect for summer picnics, but the recipe is easily halved.

---

2 kirby cucumbers, well scrubbed and cut into ¼-inch pieces
1½ teaspoons salt
¾ cup chicken stock preferably homemade (page 212), or
 low-sodium canned broth
6 tablespoons fresh lemon juice
3 tablespoons extra-virgin olive oil
¼ teaspoon freshly ground black pepper
1 pound dried orzo
6 ripe medium plum tomatoes, seeded and chopped into
 ¼-inch pieces
1 cup chopped fresh parsley
4 scallions, chopped
¼ cup chopped fresh mint or 1 tablespoon dried mint

---

1. In a medium bowl, toss the cucumbers with 1 teaspoon of the salt. Let stand 30 minutes. Drain, rinse under cold water, drain again, and pat dry with paper towels. Set aside.

2. In a medium bowl, whisk the chicken stock, lemon juice, olive oil, the remaining ½ teaspoon salt, and the pepper until combined. Set aside.

3. In a large pot of boiling salted water, cook the pasta until barely tender, about 5 minutes. Drain, rinse under cold water until completely cooled, and drain well. Transfer to a large bowl.

4. Add the cucumbers, tomatoes, parsley, scallions, and mint. Drizzle with half of the dressing and toss well. Cover and refrigerate for at least 1 hour, or up to 1 day. Refrigerate the remaining dressing.

5. Just before serving, add the remaining dressing to the salad and toss again. Taste and season with additional salt and pepper if needed. Serve chilled or at room temperature.

NUTRITIONAL ANALYSIS PER SERVING (BASED ON 10 SERVINGS)

CALORIES: 66 (7 percent from protein, 37 percent from carbohydrate, 55 percent from fat) • PROTEIN: 1 gram • CARBOHYDRATE: 7 grams • FAT: 4 grams • CHOLESTEROL: 0 milligrams • SODIUM: 168 milligrams

GRILLED TUNA WITH PESTO PASTA SALAD

MAKES 6 SERVINGS

This chunky mélange of pasta, tuna, and vegetables is bound to become a favorite on your picnic table. You won't miss the copious amounts of olive oil that undermine the nutritional benefits of many cold salads. If desired, substitute two six-and-a-quarter-ounce cans of tuna packed in water, drained and flaked, for the grilled tuna.

2 5-ounce tuna steaks, about ½ inch thick
1 teaspoon olive oil
½ teaspoon salt
¼ teaspoon freshly ground black pepper
8 ounces dried medium pasta shells
½ pint cherry tomatoes, halved
1 medium zucchini, well scrubbed, halved lengthwise, and
  cut into ¼-inch-thick half-moons
2 celery ribs, cut into ¼-inch-thick slices
½ cup Lean Pesto (page 88)
⅓ cup low-sodium tomato vegetable juice blend
2 tablespoons red wine vinegar

1. Build a hot fire in a charcoal grill.

2. Brush both sides of the tuna steaks lightly with the oil, then sprinkle with ¼ teaspoon of the salt and ⅛ teaspoon of the pepper. Grill the tuna, turning once, until medium-rare, about 4 minutes total (or cook it to your desired doneness). Cool slightly, then chop into ½-inch pieces, cover, and refrigerate.

3. Meanwhile, in a large pot of boiling salted water, cook the pasta until just tender, about 8 minutes. Drain, rinse under cold water until completely cooled, and drain well. Transfer to a large bowl. Stir in the cherry tomatoes, zucchini, and celery, and toss well.

In a medium bowl, whisk together the pesto, vegetable juice, vinegar, d the remaining ¼ teaspoon salt and ⅛ teaspoon pepper. Add half the pesto dressing to the pasta and mix well. Cover and refrigerate un- l chilled, at least 1 hour, or up to 8 hours. Refrigerate the remaining essing.

. Just before serving, add the tuna and remaining dressing to the salad d toss again. Taste and season with additional salt and pepper if needed. rve chilled.

NUTRITIONAL ANALYSIS PER SERVING

CALORIES: 264 (29 percent from protein, 54 percent from carbohydrate, 17 percent from fat) • PROTEIN: 19 grams • CARBOHYDRATE: 35 grams • FAT: 5 grams • CHOLESTEROL: 22 milligrams • SODIUM: 331 milligrams

TWO-TOMATO PASTA SALAD

MAKES 6 TO 8 SERVINGS

The intense flavor of the sun-dried tomato pesto is accented by the tan of fresh tomatoes. When you have the pesto on hand, this is a breeze t prepare, making it perfect for lazy summer lunches or suppers.

½ cup Sun-dried Tomato Pesto (page 189)
1 cup low-sodium tomato-vegetable juice blend
1 tablespoon red wine vinegar
1 pound dried tubular pasta, such as penne
1 pint cherry tomatoes, halved
½ cup chopped fresh basil
Salt to taste
Freshly ground black pepper, to taste

---

1. In a medium bowl, whisk together the pesto, vegetable juice, anc vinegar. Set aside.

2. In a large pot of boiling salted water, cook the pasta until barely tender, about 8 minutes. Drain, rinse under cold water until completely cooled, and drain well. Transfer to a large bowl.

3. Add the cherry tomatoes, basil, and half of the dressing to the pasta. Toss well, cover, and refrigerate until chilled, at least 1 hour, or up to 1 day.

4. Just before serving, toss the salad with the remaining dressing. Taste and season with salt and pepper if needed. Serve chilled or at room temperature.

NUTRITIONAL ANALYSIS PER SERVING (BASED ON 8 SERVINGS)
CALORIES: 262 (13 percent from protein, 81 percent from carbohydrate, 6 percent from fat) •
PROTEIN: 9 grams • CARBOHYDRATE: 53 grams • FAT: 2 grams • CHOLESTEROL: 0 milligrams •
SODIUM: 88 milligrams

COUSCOUS SALAD WITH CITRUS-MINT VINAIGRETTE

MAKES ABOUT 1 CUP VINAIGRETTE; 6 TO 8 SERVINGS

———

This colorful, refreshing salad has graced many of my buffet tables. It contains quite a collection of spices, but they combine beautifully to make an extraordinary Moroccan-inspired low-fat dressing.

———

CITRUS-MINT VINAIGRETTE

½ cup chicken stock, preferably homemade (page 212), or
  low-sodium canned broth
Grated zest of 1 large orange
¼ cup fresh lemon juice
3 tablespoons fresh orange juice
2 tablespoons extra-virgin olive oil
1 tablespoon chopped fresh mint or 1 teaspoon dried mint
½ teaspoon ground cumin
¼ teaspoon ground cinnamon
¼ teaspoon turmeric
½ teaspoon salt, or more to taste
⅛ teaspoon cayenne pepper, or more to taste

2¼ cups water
½ teaspoon salt
1 10-ounce box quick-cooking couscous
2 medium carrots, cut into ¼-inch cubes
1 16-ounce can garbanzo beans (chick-peas), drained and rinsed
1 medium zucchini, well scrubbed and cut into ¼-inch cubes
3 scallions, finely chopped
½ cup raisins

———

1. Make the citrus vinaigrette: In a medium bowl, whisk together the stock, orange zest and juice, lemon juice, oil, mint, cumin, cinnamon, turmeric, salt, and cayenne. Set aside.

(continued)

2. In a medium saucepan, bring the water and salt to a boil over high heat. Stir in the couscous. Immediately remove from the heat, cover tightly, and let stand for 5 minutes. Transfer the couscous to a large bowl and fluff with a fork. Cool completely.

3. In a small saucepan of boiling lightly salted water, cook the carrots for 1 minute. Drain, rinse well under cold water, and drain again.

4. Stir the carrots, garbanzo beans, zucchini, scallions, and raisins into the couscous. Drizzle with half of the citrus vinaigrette and toss well. Cover and refrigerate until chilled, at least 1 hour, or up to 1 day. Refrigerate the remaining dressing.

5. Just before serving, toss the couscous with the remaining vinaigrette. Taste and season with additional salt and cayenne pepper if needed. Serve chilled or at room temperature.

NUTRITIONAL ANALYSIS PER SERVING (BASED ON 8 SERVINGS)

CALORIES: 244 (11 percent from protein, 73 percent from carbohydrate, 16 percent from fat) • PROTEIN: 7 grams • CARBOHYDRATE: 45 grams • FAT: 4 grams • CHOLESTEROL: 0 milligrams • SODIUM: 465 milligrams

---

BUCKWHEAT NOODLE AND VEGETABLE SALAD

MAKES 8 SERVINGS

———

The resilient texture and full flavor of buckwheat noodles make them perfect for pasta salads. To be sure they retain their texture, use the authentic Japanese method for boiling the noodles. It may take a bit longer, but the results are worth the effort.

———

1 pound dried buckwheat noodles (soba)
1 large red bell pepper, stemmed, seeded, and thinly sliced
1 large cucumber, peeled, halved lengthwise, seeds removed with a
spoon, and thinly sliced into half-moons
2 medium carrots, grated
4 scallions, thinly sliced
3 tablespoons chopped fresh cilantro
⅓ cup plus 1 tablespoon chicken stock, preferably homemade
(page 212), or low-sodium canned broth
3 tablespoons low-sodium soy sauce
2 tablespoons balsamic vinegar
2 tablespoons rice vinegar
1 tablespoon dark Asian sesame oil
1 tablespoon dry sherry
1 tablespoon honey
¼ teaspoon crushed hot red pepper

1. Cook the noodles: Add the noodles, in four additions, to a large pot of briskly boiling water, stirring after each addition to keep the noodles from sticking to each other. Return the water to a full boil, then add 1 cup of cold water. When the water comes back to the boil, add another cup of cold water. Bring to a boil again, add another cup of cold water, and bring back to a full boil. Test one of the noodles for doneness; it should be just tender. If not, cook a few seconds longer. Drain the noodles, rinse under gently running cold water until completely cool, and drain well. Transfer to a large bowl.

2. Stir the red bell pepper, cucumber, carrots, scallions, and cilantro into the noodles.

3. In a medium bowl, whisk together the chicken stock, soy sauce, vinegars, sesame oil, sherry, sugar, and crushed red pepper. Add half of the dressing to the noodles and mix well. Cover and refrigerate until chilled, at least 1 hour, or up to 1 day. Refrigerate the remaining dressing.

4. When ready to serve, add the remaining dressing to the salad and toss well. Serve chilled or at room temperature.

NUTRITIONAL ANALYSIS PER SERVING

CALORIES: 241 (14 percent from protein, 77 percent from carbohydrate, 9 percent from fat) • PROTEIN: 9 grams • CARBOHYDRATE: 50 grams • FAT: 2 grams • CHOLESTEROL: 0 milligrams • SODIUM: 716 milligrams

CHICKEN AND ORZO SALAD WITH BANANA CURRY DRESSING

MAKES 2 CUPS DRESSING; 8 SERVINGS

This chicken and pasta salad is excellent luncheon fare. Banana, an un
usual addition, gives body to the zesty, slightly sweet, dressing. In fac
I like this dressing so much, I often use it on my dinner salad greens.

BANANA CURRY DRESSING

2 small bananas (about 1 cup mashed)
½ cup apple juice
2 tablespoons fresh lime juice
1 tablespoon plus 1 teaspoon curry powder, preferably Madras-style
1 tablespoon plus 1 teaspoon grated fresh ginger
½ teaspoon salt
⅛ teaspoon cayenne pepper, or more to taste

8 ounces dried orzo
3 cups cut-up cooked chicken breast meat (cut into 1-inch pieces)
2 celery ribs, chopped
1 green apple, peeled, cored, and chopped

1. Make the dressing: In a blender, blend the bananas, apple juice, lime
juice, curry powder, ginger, salt, and cayenne until smooth. Set aside.

2. In a large pot of boiling salted water, cook the pasta until barely tender,
about 5 minutes. Drain, rinse under cold water to cool completely, and
drain well. Transfer to a large bowl.

Add half of the dressing to the orzo, along with the chicken, celery,
d apple. Toss well. Cover and refrigerate until chilled, at least 1 hour,
up to 1 day. Refrigerate the remaining dressing.

Just before serving, add the remaining dressing, and season with ad-
tional salt and cayenne pepper if needed. Serve the salad chilled.

NUTRITIONAL ANALYSIS PER SERVING

CALORIES: 235 (36 percent from protein, 52 percent from carbohydrate, 12 percent from fat) •
PROTEIN: 21 grams • CARBOHYDRATE: 30 grams • FAT: 3 grams • CHOLESTEROL: 45 milligrams
• SODIUM: 118 milligrams

ASIAN VEGETABLE PASTA SALAD WITH CUCUMBER-CILANTRO DRESSING

MAKES 2 CUPS DRESSING; 6 TO 8 SERVINGS

———

The cool taste of cucumber combined with the tang of yogurt makes refreshing dressing that gives this salad a creamy character. Don't b tempted to add all of the yogurt to the blender, it will thin out too much Blend only half, and stir in the remainder.

———

CUCUMBER-CILANTRO DRESSING

1 cup plain nonfat yogurt
1 medium cucumber, scrubbed, halved lengthwise, seeds removed with a spoon, and cut into chunks
2 scallions, coarsely chopped
1 garlic clove, crushed
¼ cup chopped fresh cilantro
2 tablespoons rice vinegar
1 teaspoon salt
¼ teaspoon freshly ground black pepper

2 ounces snow peas, trimmed and cut lengthwise into thin strips
2 carrots, peeled and thinly sliced on the diagonal
1 pound dried tubular pasta, such as mostacciolli
3 scallions, thinly sliced on the diagonal
2 celery ribs, thinly sliced on the diagonal
1 red bell pepper, stemmed, seeded, and cut into thin strips

———

1. Make the dressing: In a blender, combine ½ cup of the yogurt, the cucumber, scallions, garlic, cilantro, vinegar, salt, and pepper. Pulse several times, then blend on high until smooth. Transfer to a small bowl and stir in the remaining yogurt. Set aside.

2. In a small saucepan of boiling water, blanch the snow peas and carrots for 30 seconds. Drain, rinse under cool water, and drain well. Set aside.

3. In a large pot of boiling salted water, cook the pasta until just tender, about 8 minutes. Drain, rinse under cold water until completely cooled, and drain well. Transfer to a large bowl.

4. Add the blanched carrots and snow peas, the scallions, celery, and red bell pepper to the pasta. Add half of the dressing and toss well. Cover and refrigerate until chilled, at least 1 hour, or up to 1 day.

5. Just before serving, toss the salad with the remaining dressing. Taste and season with additional salt and pepper if needed. Serve chilled or at room temperature.

NUTRITIONAL ANALYSIS PER SERVING (BASED ON 8 SERVINGS)

CALORIES: 263 (15 percent from protein, 80 percent from carbohydrate, 4 percent from fat) • PROTEIN: 10 grams • CARBOHYDRATE: 52 grams • FAT: 1 gram • CHOLESTEROL: less than 1 milligram • SODIUM: 306 milligrams

RATATOUILLE AND PENNE SALAD WITH BALSAMIC DRESSING

MAKES 3 CUPS DRESSING; 6 TO 8 SERVINGS

———

I love ratatouille, that famous blend of Mediterranean vegetables, but it is usually swimming in olive oil. For this salad, I devised a way of preparing the eggplant without using loads of fat.

———

BALSAMIC DRESSING

1 cup low-sodium tomato-vegetable juice blend
¾ cup chicken stock, preferably homemade (page 212), or
   low-sodium canned broth
⅓ cup plus 1 tablespoon balsamic vinegar
¾ cup lightly packed fresh basil
¼ cup liquid egg substitute
2 tablespoons tomato paste
1 garlic clove, minced
1 teaspoon salt
¼ teaspoon freshly ground black pepper

Nonstick vegetable cooking spray
1 medium eggplant (about 1¼ pounds), trimmed and cut into
   ¾-inch pieces
1 tablespoon olive oil
1 pound dried penne or other tubular pasta
1 pound ripe medium plum tomatoes, seeded and coarsely chopped
1 medium zucchini, well scrubbed, halved lengthwise, and cut into
   thin half-moons
1 red bell pepper, stemmed, seeded, and cut into thin strips
1 medium red onion, chopped

———

. Make the dressing: In a blender, process the vegetable juice, stock, vinegar, basil, egg substitute, tomato paste, garlic, salt, and pepper until smooth.

. Preheat the oven to 450°F. Lightly spray a baking sheet with cooking spray.

. Place the eggplant on the baking sheet in a single layer. Drizzle with the olive oil and bake, stirring once, until browned and tender, 20 to 30 minutes.

4. Meanwhile, in a large pot of boiling salted water, cook the pasta until just tender, about 8 minutes. Drain, rinse under cold water until completely cooled, and drain again. Transfer to a large bowl.

5. Add the cooked eggplant to the pasta, along with the tomatoes, zucchini, red pepper, and onion. Toss with half of the dressing. Cover and refrigerate until chilled, at least 1 hour, or up to 1 day.

6. Just before serving, toss the salad with the remaining dressing. Taste and season with additional salt and pepper if needed. Serve chilled or at room temperature.

NUTRITIONAL ANALYSIS PER SERVING (BASED ON 8 SERVINGS)

CALORIES: 79 (13 percent from protein, 62 percent from carbohydrate, 25 percent from fat) • PROTEIN: 2 grams • CARBOHYDRATE: 13 grams • FAT: 2 grams • CHOLESTEROL: 0 milligrams • SODIUM: 361 milligrams

---

COLD ORIENTAL NOODLES WITH GINGERY PEANUT DRESSING

These are very similiar to the spicy sesame noodles that are a Chinese restaurant standard—minus most of the fat. The dressing can be made ahead of time, but don't dress the noodles until you are ready to serve— they become heavy upon standing.

GINGERY PEANUT DRESSING

8 ounces firm tofu, drained
½ cup chicken stock, preferably homemade (page 212), or low-sodium canned broth
3 tablespoons evaporated skimmed milk
2 tablespoons low-sodium soy sauce
2 tablespoons unsalted natural peanut butter
2 tablespoons grated fresh ginger
2 garlic cloves, crushed
2 teaspoons sugar
¼ teaspoon crushed hot red pepper

1 pound freshly made or store-bought fresh cholesterol-free linguine
2 cups fresh bean sprouts
2 scallions, cut into very thin diagonal slices
1 celery rib, cut into very thin diagonal slices
1 carrot, coarsely grated

------

1. Make the dressing: In a blender, process the tofu, stock, evaporated skimmed milk, soy sauce, peanut butter, ginger, garlic, sugar, and crushed red pepper until smooth. Set aside.

2. In a large pot of boiling salted water, cook the pasta until just tender, 2 to 3 minutes. Drain, rinse under gently running cold water until completely cooled, and drain again. Transfer to a medium bowl.

3. Immediately add the dressing to the noodles and toss well. Transfer to individual bowls and serve immediately with bowls of the bean sprouts, scallions, celery, and carrots passed on the side, so guests can choose their own toppings.

NUTRITIONAL ANALYSIS PER SERVING (BASED ON 6 SERVINGS)

CALORIES: 355 (20 percent from protein, 58 percent from carbohydrate, 22 percent from fat) • PROTEIN: 18 grams • CARBOHYDRATE: 52 grams • FAT: 9 grams • CHOLESTEROL: less than 1 milligram • SODIUM: 310 milligrams

FARM STAND PASTA SALAD WITH TOMATO-SHERRY DRESSING

MAKES ABOUT 1¾ CUPS DRESSING; 6 TO 8 SERVINGS

———

One summer afternoon, I came home with an armful of August's bounty and was inspired to make this pasta salad for supper. We thought we weren't hungry (it was a hot evening), but when we had finished, we didn't have a single bite left over. The dressing is a simple puree of tomatoes, sherry vinegar (available at specialty food stores), shallot, and garlic. Sherry vinegar is only mildly acidic; if you use red wine vinegar, add the optional sugar to balance its acidity.

———

TOMATO-SHERRY DRESSING

1 pound ripe plum tomatoes, halved and seeded
3 tablespoons sherry vinegar or red wine vinegar
1 teaspoon sugar (optional)
1 shallot, chopped
1 garlic clove, crushed
¼ teaspoon salt
¼ teaspoon freshly ground black pepper

1 pound dried rotini or other spiral pasta
2 cups fresh or defrosted frozen corn kernels
1 medium zucchini, well scrubbed, halved lengthwise, and cut into
  ¼-inch-thick half-moons
1 medium red bell pepper, stemmed, seeded, and thinly sliced
¼ cup chopped fresh dill

———

1. Make the dressing: In a blender, process the tomatoes, vinegar, optional sugar, shallot, garlic, salt, and pepper until smooth. Set aside.

2. In a large pot of boiling salted water, cook the pasta until just tender, about 8 minutes. Drain, rinse under cold water until completely cooled, and drain well. Transfer to a large bowl.

3. Add the corn, zucchini, bell pepper, and dill to the pasta. Add half of the dressing, and toss well. Cover and refrigerate until chilled, at least 1 hour or up to 1 day.

4. Just before serving, toss the salad with the remaining dressing. Taste and season with additional salt and pepper if needed. Serve chilled or at room temperature.

NUTRITIONAL ANALYSIS PER SERVING (BASED ON 8 SERVINGS)

CALORIES: 285 (13 percent from protein, 82 percent from carbohydrate, 4 percent from fat) • PROTEIN: 10 grams • CARBOHYDRATE: 60 grams • FAT: 1 gram • CHOLESTEROL: 0 milligrams • SODIUM: 78 milligrams

GRILLED SHRIMP AND RADIATORE SALAD WITH CILANTRO-TOMATILLO PESTO

MAKES ABOUT 1¾ CUPS PESTO; 8 SERVINGS

———

Cilantro is an herb that few people are ambivalent about—either you love it or hate it. I had always considered myself a nonenthusiast, until I devised this pungent pesto. You will probably find yourself making this lovely green dressing to pour onto green salads or toss with hot pasta.

———

CILANTRO-TOMATILLO PESTO

1 12-ounce can tomatillos, drained and rinsed
1 cup fresh cilantro leaves
1 cup nonfat cottage cheese
2 scallions, chopped
1 hot green chile pepper, such as jalapeño, seeded and
  finely chopped (or to taste)
1 garlic clove, minced
¼ teaspoon salt

1 pound medium shrimp, peeled and deveined
2 tablespoons fresh lime juice
1 teaspoon chili powder
¼ teaspoon salt
1 pound dried radiatore or other curly short pasta
1 red bell pepper, stemmed, seeded, and chopped

4 long bamboo skewers, soaked in water for 30 minutes
  and drained

———

1. Make the pesto: In a food processor fitted with the metal blade or a blender, process the tomatillos, cilantro, cottage cheese, scallions, chile pepper, garlic, and salt until smooth. Set aside. (The pesto can be made up to 2 days ahead, covered, and refrigerated.)

2. Build a hot fire in a charcoal grill or preheat a gas grill on "high."

3. In a medium bowl, toss the shrimp with the lime juice, chili powder, and salt. Let stand for 15 minutes.

4. Drain the shrimp, reserving the marinade. Thread 6 shrimp onto each bamboo skewer by folding each shrimp into its natural "C" shape, and spearing the shrimp through the top and bottom of the "C" to hold its shape. (This keeps the shrimp from rotating on the skewer when turned.)

5. Brush the grill grate with vegetable oil. Grill the shrimp, turning once and basting with the reserved marinade, until just pink and firm, about 4 minutes total. Cool the shrimp completely. Remove the skewers, cover, and refrigerate. (The shrimp can also be broiled under a preheated broiler turning once, for about 4 minutes.)

6. In a large pot of boiling salted water, cook the pasta until just tender, about 8 minutes. Drain, rinse under cold water until completely cooled, and drain again. Transfer the pasta to a large bowl.

7. Add the shrimp and bell pepper to the pasta. Add half of the pesto, and toss well. Cover and refrigerate for at least 1 hour, or up to 8 hours. Refrigerate the remaining pesto.

8. Just before serving, add the remaining pesto to the salad and toss again. Taste and season with additional salt and pepper if needed. Serve chilled.

Note: If your supermarket doesn't carry cilantro (also called Chinese parsley or coriander), look for it at Asian or Hispanic markets. Tomatillos, canned or fresh, are found at Hispanic markets. You can substitute 1 pound of fresh tomatillos, husks removed, for the canned in this recipe. To prepare the fresh tomatillos, simmer them in a medium saucepan of lightly salted water over medium-low heat until just tender, but not bursting, about 5 minutes. Drain well. (You can also substitute one 16-ounce can of tomatoes, drained, for the tomatillos to make a different pesto.)

NUTRITIONAL ANALYSIS PER SERVING

CALORIES: 302 (29 percent from protein, 66 percent from carbohydrate, 5 percent from fat) • PROTEIN: 21 grams • CARBOHYDRATE: 49 grams • FAT: 2 grams • CHOLESTEROL: 88 milligrams • SODIUM: 255 milligrams

MAIL-ORDER SOURCES

For whole-grain and semolina flours:

The Baker's Catalogue (King Arthur Flour)
RR 2, Box 56
Norwich, VT 05055
1-800-827-6836

For hand-cranked pasta machines, manual-extruder machines, and flavoring oils:

Williams-Sonoma
P.O. Box 7456
San Francisco, CA 94120-7456
415-421-4242

INDEX

Sauces (continued)
tequila-spiked tomato, clams on
vermicelli in, 150–151
Thai chicken-basil, with linguine, 208–
209
tomato-vodka, spaghetti with, 115–116
turkey ragù on fettuccine, 100–101
vegetable, egg noodles with Peking
turkey and, 204–205
white wine, clams and spaghetti in, 106–
107
Sausage, turkey, see Turkey sausage
Scallion pancake pasta:
electric machine method, 82
hand method, 58
Scallops:
in rosemary-vermouth sauce on linguine,
160–161
sautéed with confetti vegetables and
linguine, 162–163
Semolina, 19
bright beet pasta, hand method, 41
and egg pasta, traditional, electric
machine method, 73–74
and egg pasta, traditional, hand method,
35
emerald spinach pasta, hand method, 40
minted zucchini pasta, hand method, 44
pasta classica, hand method, 36
pesto pasta, hand method, 46
tomato blush pasta, hand method, 38–39
Servings, recommended daily, 4
Shallots, 23
Shapes, pasta, 13–14, 33
Shellfish:
and mushroom lasagne, 128–130
San Francisco cio-pasta, 225–226
see also specific shellfish
Shells:
grilled tuna with pesto, salad, 230–231
shrimp-and-spinach-stuffed, 133–134
swordfish with sun-dried tomato pesto
on, 148
Sherry-tomato dressing, 244–245
Sherry vinegar, 25
Shrimp:
grilled, and radiatore salad with cilantro-
tomatillo pesto, 246–247
sizzling orange, vermicelli with, 163–164
spicy Cajun, on linguine, 140–141
-and-spinach-stuffed shells, 133–134
stir-fried Thai rice noodles with tofu and,
199–200
with tomatoes and corn on linguine,
149–150
Sicilian tuna and tomato pasta, 142

Skillets, nonstick, 21
Snap peas:
sugar, and herb pasta, springtime, 190–
191
turkey, and red peppers with penne,
158–159
Soba (buckwheat noodles), and vegetable
salad, 234–235
Soups, 211–226
chicken stock, 212–213
fish and pasta, Niçoise, 214–215
fish stock, 214–215
garlic-vegetable, with whole wheat
noodles, 220–221
Italian sausage and peppers, 223–224
Mexican tomato-noodle, 212–213
pastas for, 13–14
quick pasta and bean, 216–217
San Francisco cio-pasta, 225–226
vegetable, pesto, and pasta, 218–219
vegetable stock, 220–221
Vietnamese beef and cellophane noodle,
206–207
vineyard minestrone, 222–223
Sources, mail-order, 249
Sour cream alternative, nonfat, 18
Spaghetti, 13
and clams in white wine sauce, 106–
107
oven-baked turkey-spinach meatballs and,
96–97
peperonata, 170–171
with salsa cruda, 166–167
Sicilian tuna and tomato, 142
with sun-dried tomato pesto, 189–190
today's turkey tetrazzini, 136–137
with tomato-vodka sauce, 115–116
white beans and tomatoes with, 156–
157
Spelt, 19, 20
pasta, electric machine method, 78
pasta, hand method, 63
Spinach:
emerald green pasta, electric machine
method, 81
emerald pasta, hand method, 39–40
pasta "pie," 124–125
-and-shrimp-stuffed shells, 133–134
-turkey meatballs and spaghetti, 96–97
Stocks:
chicken, 212–213
fish, 214–215
vegetable, 220–221
Sun-dried tomato(es), 23
artichoke, and turkey ham fettuccine,
154–155

Whole wheat:
noodles, garlic-vegetable soup with, 220–221
pasta, electric machine method, 77–78
pasta, hand method, 62–63
Wine, red, vineyard minestrone, 222–223
Wine, white, sauce, clams and spaghetti in, 106–107

Yogurt chicken sauce, Madras, fettuccine with, 143–144

Ziti:
broccoli rabe and sausage with, 108–10⦋
with Moroccan-spiced baked eggplant sauce, 174–175
Zucchini:
coins with bucatini, 180–181
and corn filling for Mexican manicotti, 131–132
and lamb pasticcio, Greek, 118–119
minted pasta, hand method, 44
vegetarian lasagne, 176–177